# ROI MARKETING

## The New Performance Standard

Pablo Turletti

Copyright © 2014 **Authored By Pablo Turletti**
All rights reserved.

ISBN 10: **978 1493759293**
ISBN 13: **1493759299**

# Contents

Preface     6

Acknowledgments     7

About ROI Marketing Institute     8

About The Author     10

Introduction     11

**Part 1**     **Why This Is Important**

*Chapter I*    *Marketing Accountability: A Critical Issue*

    Based on a True Story     14
    Introduction     18
    What Can You Expect from This Book?     24
    Why Is It Necessary?     27
    Closing Points     29

*Chapter II*    *Measurement and Evaluation in Marketing*

    Based on a True Story     30
    About Measuring ROI in Marketing     32
    What Is ROI Marketing?     36
    ROI Marketing Guidelines     39
    Barriers to Implementing ROI Marketing     41
    Closing Points     46

## Chapter III  The ROI Marketing Matrix: The Theory behind It

| | |
|---|---|
| Based on a True Story | 47 |
| Introduction to the ROI Marketing Matrix | 49 |
| Evaluating Levels & Measuring Dimensions | 54 |
| The ROI Marketing Cascade | 57 |
| About Business Alignment and Objectives | 58 |
| Requirements for Objectives | 65 |
| About Project Planning | 66 |
| Does My Project Make Sense from an ROI Perspective? ROI Sensitivity Analysis | 68 |
| Putting It All Together—the ROI Marketing Ladder | 74 |
| About Data Collection | 79 |
| Translating Communications Results into Business Variables | 88 |
| Closing Points | 102 |

## Part 2    ROI Marketing Matrix: How to Use It

### Chapter IV: ROI Marketing from Theory to Practice

| | |
|---|---|
| Overview | 104 |
| How Close Is My Company to Implementing ROI Marketing | 108 |
| Business Alignment | 110 |
| Setting Objectives | 113 |
| Marketing Strategy | 123 |
| Marketing Tactics | 124 |
| ROI Sensitivity Analysis | 129 |
| Data Collection | 134 |

|   |   |
|---|---|
| Relating Effects | 137 |
| Converting to Money | 146 |
| ROI Calculation | 149 |
| Conclusions | 156 |

**Appendix A: How to Get Started**     160

## Preface

Marketing is a very inexact discipline. It depends on perceptions and behaviors that are triggered by a very broad set of parameters that range from emotional to rational and functional appreciations. Decision patterns are as varied as the people behind them. In addition, marketing also has a stigma associated with it. Politics, sports…and marketing are the three things everybody thinks he or she has the right to talk and draw conclusions about. No one in a company would dare to question an engineer about the type of machine he or she selected to best suit the production needs of a given brand. No one would dare to question the CFO about his or her accounting criteria. However, when the new marketing campaign is presented to the board, everybody feels it is within his or her rights to question the CMO about his or her assertions.

Inaccuracy and the fact that everybody in the company feels qualified to discuss or question plans make marketing a vulnerable and often unappreciated discipline within many businesses.

If marketing becomes accountable, there is a very clear way to give those in marketing a voice within the business. If business results come from marketing and these are demonstrated, it will be more difficult for marketers to be questioned in the planning stages with any solid basis other than appreciation.

Calculating the return on any investment is straightforward. It is necessary to divide the contribution (sometimes referred to as the *gross margin* or *net revenue*) by the investment and multiply it by one hundred to get the percentage; the difficulty in marketing lies in defining what the contribution is and figuring out how to obtain the data that will determine it. An accessible method of determining the net contribution of a marketing project has been the Holy Grail for many years. Everyone desires it, but nobody can reach it—at least not with certain consensus and credibility.

The methodology presented in this book (the ROI Marketing Matrix) aims to satisfy this need from a broad point of view, which will cover all possible marketing projects in any type of business. It is general and applicable to most cases. The results obtained from the use of the methodology will have different degrees of accuracy, from total certainty to an estimated approximation. However, marketers should not be deceived by the latter. The rigor implemented by the methodology and a disciplined practice will bring credibility and robustness to even the broadest of estimations. Furthermore, it is always much better to have an estimation with a gauged probability of occurrence than to have no idea at all about the final impact of marketing on the business.

**Acknowledgments**

No intellectual work can be the result of one person alone. This book is no exception. Dozens of project experiences with clients over almost two decades were needed to give birth to the ROI Marketing Matrix. First and foremost goes this thank mention to all those clients that endured the process and were open to take a new approach. This work was also possible thank to the staff people that worked on each and every one of those projects trying to understand, and supporting at the same time, a process that was not always that clear. In 2005 I started my executive education at IESE Business School, this was a landmark on the intellectual revolution that this institution generated in me, thank you also to all the staff and professors of the global Executive MBA Program. Finally, no business related matter could come across anybody's brain if that brain is not happy, loved and balanced. My wife Natalia and my sons Mateo and Lucas are the ones responsible for this. To them my eternal love, devotion, and dedication.

**About the ROI Marketing Institute**

Responding to an always increasing number of organizations searching for ways to make marketing accountable, the ROI Marketing Institute (www.roimarketinginstitute.com) was founded to help companies and all sorts of institutions to implement ROI Marketing within their structures, processes, and procedures. Its tools and services to achieve this goal are:

- Training—Through a customized set of courses, the ROI Marketing Institute can prepare marketing teams to adapt their processes and procedures to

measure the financial return of their marketing investments.
- Certification—the ROI Marketing Institute is the only institution worldwide that can award official ROI Marketing Champion certification to professionals and institutions attesting ROI Marketing Matrix competencies and knowledge that has been demonstrated in the field along with a proven capability to sustain them over time. Certifications add great value to professionals' résumés and send a clear message to investors and shareholders about a given business's cash-flow management.
- System Implementation—For the most committed organizations, the ROI Marketing Institute and its team of technicians can design, program, and start up in-house systems that will help the organization to automate the process of measuring the return of marketing investments.
- Consulting—The ROI Marketing Institute operates with a network of international partners and analysts who can carry out ROI studies for marketing projects and campaigns for all sorts of organizations around the world.

# About the Author

Pablo Turletti is an internationally recognized expert on marketing strategy, implementation, and results evaluation. He is a corporate executive with an entrepreneurial mind capable of taking marketing to levels beyond communication. During his more than twenty years of experience, he has lived on four different continents and worked for companies, nonprofits, and governmental organizations in many different sectors. He knows how to leverage large corporations marketing budgets in order to deliver communication and business results. Mr. Turletti became a reputed speaker and consultant able to show the contribution of marketing to the businesses at different levels. Author of several articles, Turletti has also conducted workshops, given conference presentations and guest lectures, and consulted on projects around the world. He is the creator of the ROI Marketing Matrix and currently sits as the CEO and managing director of the ROI Marketing Institute, headquartered I Switzerland. He can be reached at pablo.turletti@roimarketinginstitute.com.

# Introduction

This book is arranged in two parts for easy reading and review.

The first part "Why This Is Important," offers an argument for the importance of marketing accountability, starting with a real-life example, with the aim of pointing out the principles and goals of each part of the methodology developed. It continues with a detailed explanation of the fundamentals behind the ROI Marketing Matrix, issues to pay attention to, and matters to take care of during an evaluation process. It covers and conveys concepts like the ROI Marketing Cascade, the ROI Marketing Ladder, and the ROI Sensitivity Analysis. It walks readers systematically through the methodology with numeric examples.

Part 2, "The ROI Marketing Matrix: How to Use It," explains in detail how independent and/or combined marketing projects are evaluated following the ROI Marketing Matrix. It shows, through examples, how information is collected and used in such a way that measuring and evaluating can become a standard practice in each and every marketing department.

Each part is arranged in a reader-friendly format. Chapters are short and get straight to the point. Each contains different questions the chapter is aiming to answer, the methodology principle/part that applies to the case, and, in part 1, a short true story that clearly demonstrates the use or need for the methodology. For reasons of confidentiality, in some cases, whenever actual numbers are mentioned, the companies' names have been changed, and whenever actual companies are mentioned, the real figures are altered.

At the end of each chapter, there is a bulleted list of closing points, which can be used as a quick reference for future consultation and easy implementation.

# Part 1
# Why This Is Important

# Chapter I
# Marketing Accountability: A Critical Issue

## Based on a True Story

At 8:00 a.m. on the morning of October 10, the fresh air of the early fall day gave Javier a burst of life as he walked down from the parking lot to his office under the usual crisp blue sky of Madrid. A great day…

Javier Moreno was the VP of marketing for RoiCo Inc., a fast-moving consumer goods manufacturer, struggling for cash while fighting for a dairy products market share and progressively losing to the distribution brands in the always sensitive-to-price market of Spain. Javier and his team had been working for some weeks to develop the marketing plan for the upcoming year, and today was the day he was to present it to the general manager and two members of the board.

He was a bit nervous, but he knew he and his marketing team had done their homework. They had set a sound strategy, with clear communications objectives, showing the different projects that were going to contribute to achieving their objectives, a detailed budget, and a description of how these projects were going to impact the market share, the share of voice, and the share of stomach.

They even had a creative concept and a mock-up of an ad that would clearly demonstrate what they were talking about (although he was a bit concerned by the fact that neither the board members nor the general manager had a marketing background. Would they *really* understand it?)

Carla, the receptionist, offered her usual bright smile to welcome him from behind a four-meter-long white reception desk, which had an engraved statement on the front that read: "RoiCo, helping to build the present and the future through our products."

As he exited the elevator on his way to his desk, he was greeted by his team with thumbs-up and fist-bumps, showing their support and encouragement.

Javier left his coat on the chair and, without sitting down, opened his laptop, made sure the presentation was open, checked that no slides were missing, and having no need to read any of the contents (after all those weeks of work, he knew it by heart), left the presentation open, and grabbed the computer, already in motion toward the largest meeting room of the company. On the way, he wondered, *There are only going to be four people; why do they always have to pick the largest room, which fits twenty?* and then thought, *I hope nobody took the remote for the projector.*

Jack Walker was the general manager of RoiCo. He had been sent from the company headquarters in Amsterdam. He was already in the room, standing next to the coffee machine with Catherine Bourdeaux and Matteo Duretti, the two board members. In the middle, between the door where Javier was entering and them, was a huge mahogany table as long as the reception desk but dark, shiny, and certainly "classier."

"Hi, Javier," Jack greeted him with an open, honest smile.

"Hola," said Javier. "I apologize for being late."

"No way, Javier; you're right on time. We came in a bit early to have a quick chat before hearing your presentation."

*What was the chat about?* Javier wondered as he approached the front of the table and positioned himself next to the connection to the projector. He was relieved to see the remote was there…

They all sat down, coffee mugs in hand, and Javier started his opening speech with a question: "What can and should we expect from our marketing for next year?"

His series of slides and videos was having a great effect on the audience. Javier could sense how much they really liked what he was presenting. Enthusiasm bloomed on both sides.

They all liked the creative concept, as it was not only eye-catching and emotionally compelling, but it also portrayed the core messages and, most important, it aligned with the business strategy perfectly.

Javier proceeded to describe how the marketing strategy was going to be implemented, the overall core projects that had been planned, and the timing of execution. Everything was going smoothly, and Javier knew he had them right where he wanted them, enthusiastically listening (nobody was using a mobile to text anybody) and awake.

When he came to the budget part, Javier knew he was on the high side. It was a customary practice to inflate the budgets so when the cuts came—and they always did and were expected to by default—the final resulting budget would be exactly what he needed or, if he were lucky, even more. The baseline was last year's budget, although savings and cuts were pushing it downward.

With the requested budget, Javier was planning to pay for the media campaign and to execute a series of events, point-of-sale activities, social media activities, and a direct marketing campaign that would bring in the input needed to achieve the objectives in terms of awareness, product launching, and the share of voice with the hope of maintaining or gaining market share and share of stomach.

It was clear and set in writing, and they liked it. Javier's presentation closed with a timid but honest applause of approval from the three attendees. Jack Walker opened the interaction.

"Thank you, Javier. You know that we have been going through some tough years. The board has asked the management team to keep our ratios so as not to lose value on the stock. With declining sales, we are forced to continue with the cost cuts and savings. I am afraid you are aware of the problems we are having with the unions, so for us, it is literally impossible to lay off more people. Right now, the only solution we have, in order to avoid cutting down on quality, is to reduce our marketing budget. I am sure you understand. So there might be a need to adjust part of your plan."

"No problem," replied Javier while thinking, *Business as usual...*

Then, suddenly, clouds appeared under the guise of a question asked by Catherine Bourdeaux. "It was a brilliant and inspiring presentation, Javier; thank you very much. But how much money is this marketing campaign going to generate for the business?"

Javier didn't blink. Although he did not have a concrete answer, he went along with the estimation they had somehow prepared based on the expected results of the campaign. Internally, however, he wished he had an indisputable answer...

## Introduction

The perception of marketing as an expense has grown over the last five to ten years. The worldwide economic crisis enhanced that feeling. The need to become more efficient and cut costs made marketing expenditures permanently more volatile, as they were revalued and questioned. Marketing plans are constantly revised, and marketing budgets are treated as an adjustment variable at the corporate level.

But marketing is as much a relevant and indispensable component of every business as finance, the supply chain, and human resources. Companies often measure the financial return of their positive cash flows, the benefits of their supply chain, and the productivity of their labor force. Very seldom do organizations determine, in monetary terms, the accountability of their marketing efforts. In a broad sense, they do; they gauge the variation of sales attributed to gross rating points (GRPs) or the inputs generated by any given project, such as participation at events, affiliation, et cetera. But certainly most fail to evaluate the opportunity cost of their different marketing projects and campaigns (including those linked to the so far most accepted measurement standard: the GRP), as well as the real return (not just the sales variation) of investments, and worst of all, most attempts fail to show a direct cause-effect relation.

This book aims to demonstrate that most (if not all) marketing projects and campaign contributions to the advertiser's business can be measured in monetary terms; that marketing is an investment and as such, we should be able to determine its return; that marketing returns should be measured quantitatively; and that for most marketing investments, there is a way to calculate the ROI in cash value. Marketing has traditionally been, and it will forever be, a discipline of communication; companies communicate about their brand identity, their messages, their offers of products and services, their promotions, their commitments to social and environmental sustainability, their information to investors—and the list continues.

Marketing key performance indicators (KPIs) have traditionally been linked to this communication world in terms of their project/campaign inputs, including but not limited to: GRPs, impacts, visits to a website, attendance at an event, responses to direct marketing efforts, affiliation, adherence, recall, awareness, and so on. But where is the link between marketing and business? While in finance, the link to the business shows in the balance sheet and profit and loss (P&L), and in human resources, it is evident in productivity indexes, where is the link to the business shown for marketing? Arguably, many marketers could say that if you stop doing marketing, you will definitively see the impact on business, and that is true, but this does not mean that we use our marketing investments efficiently; furthermore, it does not link the effects directly to the cause. It does not show whether we could have achieved the same results with less investment or the potential marginal contribution of extra investments. It also does not provide any value for deciding on future investments. Even the recently coined term *performance marketing*, while results-driven, fails to show the contribution of marketing to the business in a quantitative fashion.

ROI Marketing represents a standard by which all marketing efforts—advertising, direct marketing, digital marketing, grassroots campaigns, events, POS marketing, and so on—can be linked to the business. ROI

Marketing shows not only the contribution and direct link to the business of marketing investments in cash; it also links its contribution to a budget. By using ROI Marketing, while keeping the essence of marketing in communication, companies will be bringing marketing directly into the bottom line reliably, accountably, and with plenty of resources to plan for future investments. Marketing budgets will be considered as investments rather than as an adjustable variable or simply a cost.

ROI Marketing is the new performance measurement standard. Regardless of the industry you are in or the marketing discipline you work on, the ROI Marketing Matrix presented in this book offers a unique, cross-sector, cross-functional, and reliable way to show the contribution of marketing to corporate communication and to business in an accountable fashion—in cash.

We cannot start talking about ROI Marketing without first considering each term separately.

It is not very well established when the term *return on investment* (*ROI*) was first used, but we can certainly state that it was born in the business environment. Since the exchange method of payment became monetary, people started to search for surpluses and bartering soon became a secondary means of transaction. People started to use their productive resources not only for subsistence but also expecting to obtain, after a given period, a surplus. This "surplus" is the expected extra money that one obtained after discounting the cost of using those resources. The use of this money with the expectation of a return could be defined as the first investment.

Basically, ROI implies, necessarily, the use of money during a time to obtain more money than was originally used. Return on investment represents money—only money...

The origins of marketing are no better defined. If we consider marketing a form of communication that generates an expectation (rational or emotional) aimed to produce an action, Adam and Eve are our first marketers. If we more rigorously relate the term to its etymology, marketing began to appear almost at the same time as ROI. If people were looking to obtain a return of money used, they had to generate certain expectations on somebody else who was willing to pay the extra money expected by the first, in exchange for the benefit of meeting the expectation by the second one. To generate these expectations, it was, and still is, necessary to communicate with a final result that will ultimately become an act of purchase or barter.

ROI and marketing are naturally linked by their economic origin and as part of the same transaction. Why is it then that while most other business-related topics, such as finance, human resources, and logistics, pose no difficulties when it comes to quantifying their contribution to the business in money, marketing has always been lagging behind? The response lies perhaps in the fact that while the previously mentioned areas have measurable variables (interest, productivity, inventory, et cetera) within which we can find a direct cause-effect link between what you use and what you get converted to money, marketing, in most cases, struggles to achieve this direct cause-effect connection.

Consider the most broadly used marketing media: TV advertising. Literally billions of euros and dollars are spent worldwide in advertising on TV every year. The standard measurable variable of money used is GRP (gross rating point). As marketers know, GRP measures the amount of target audience supposedly reached through the spot emission or "air time." But in most cases, marketers fail to obtain and general management does not demand a direct connection to the impact of such investments on the business (generally sales). It is assumed, considering the classical theory, that keeping all other elements of the marketing mix still (product, price, and placement), the variation in sales can be attributed to advertising, and in some cases, that may hold true. However, over the last twenty years, marketing and marketers have undergone a deep transformation, which includes the appearance of new media and channels. A complete revolution in consumer behavior began and is still occurring, while there is also an incredible increase in the speed of changes and the evolution of production and pricing models. The relative weight of advertising started to diminish (a trend confirmed by more than fifteen years of decreasing relative investments in conventional media advertising, favoring other means of communication, such as grassroots efforts, events, digital marketing, and social media campaigns, just to name a few) and with it, the relevance of the only generally accepted standard of measurement, the GRP. After all, GRPs are something you buy rather than something you get out of your marketing investments.

Over the last decade, marketers have been more incisively facing the challenge of demonstrating the value of marketing for the business and struggling to show that value in monetary terms. Many ways of measuring return appeared: return on emotions, return on assets, return on impacts, et cetera, but all of them fail to show marketing accountability.

This book proposes an answer to this relevant and broadly presented matter. If marketing and ROI are linked by their economic/financial nature and there is a growing need to connect them and show the contribution of all marketing-related projects and campaigns, the ROI Marketing Matrix we are going to introduce and the way we, marketers, use it will bring the possibility of monetizing them all, generating, in the process, a new marketing-unique KPI standard.

**What Can You Expect from This Book?**

This book is a basic guide for anyone involved in creating, producing, and implementing any type of marketing project or campaign. Consumers have changed, and the world of business has been radically altered as well. The speed of change is continuously increasing, and experience in any specific type of marketing, field, channel, or media is a relatively diminishing value. By the time a marketer becomes an "expert" in any media or channel, this channel or media has changed or new ones have appeared, forcing professionals to "relearn" and in many cases start from scratch. This book addresses a results-based approach that begins with the end in mind and collects data in several dimensions, from qualitative to quantitative, not only from the communication/message point of view but also from the business impact and return standpoint. These data do answer several questions:

- What do they think about my company, brand, and/or product?
- What is the promise our products and brands are projecting to the market?
- What do they know about my company, brand, and/or product?
- How much do they know about it?
- Do they know where to buy it and how to use it?
- What do I want them to do with what they think and know about my company, brand, and/or product?
- What are the results of our call to action?
- What impact does what they do have on my sales and costs?
- If I cannot measure the impact on sales or costs, how can I define the value as an intangible?
- Are we really making money (profit, not just revenue) with our marketing projects?

In this book, you will see how to set objectives based on different aspects of communication- and business-related matters, establish key performance indicators (KPIs) that can unequivocally show us the sought-after cause-effect relation, and collect and analyze the data to obtain the impact, not only in communication, but also in the business, in a tangible way, in ROI, in *money*.

We propose a matrix that should allow marketers, regardless of the type of project they are handling—events, direct marketing, grassroots, or advertising—to obtain the ROI (money) generated by each one of those projects or for all of them as a campaign. This approach changes the focus from activity-based to results-based, from communication-based to communication- and business-impact-based, and from input-based (GRP, OTS, et cetera) to output (ROI).

The question then diverts from how many GRP you bought, direct responses, unique visitors to a website, customer satisfaction, "likes" in Facebook, click-through ratio (CTR), opportunity to see (OTS), audience, et cetera (all activity-based and input-related measures) to "What's the ROI?" This is just one type of comparable, usable, extendable data; it is a number, representing money (not value) that will be in the pockets of the business and that the business can use, for instance, at the end of the month to pay its payroll.

In this book, we aim to present a method focused on building a credible process that generates value in money that is simple, robust, feasible, accurate, and reliable. It approaches credibility in a direct way through:

 1. defined and clearly identifiable sets of data,

2. a systematic process approach, and
3. a set of standards and milestones.

The book explores the challenges of collecting data in a measurable way and linking it to monetary value. This will be an indispensable guide for marketers who seek to understand more about the bottom-line accountability of marketing-related projects and campaigns.

## Why Is It Necessary?

With the reality of economic struggles, cost-cutting policies and the need for short-term returns, accountability and efficiency must be addressed early and often in new projects and campaigns. This book shows marketing professionals and managers how to measure the success of their projects, events, campaigns, and communications initiatives (internal or external) with a standard, cross-functional, cross-media, and cross-channel profile of success, including the financial ROI.

Collectively, the output (rather than the input) measures taken from the use of the ROI Marketing Matrix presented in this book capture a profile of success, representing qualitative and quantitative data taken from different levels and dimensions, reflecting both financial and nonfinancial outcomes.

With its conservative standards and systematic approach, the ROI Marketing Matrix is CFO and CEO friendly. The results and conclusions obtained will facilitate marketers in securing funding; building support for projects and campaigns; improving processes and procedures, as well as their relationships with general management, C-level executives, and stakeholders; and dignifying the image of marketing as a discipline. An important advantage of this process is that it is dynamic and focuses on improvement while still maintaining its focus on results. If a particular project or campaign is not adding value, steps can be taken to make it successful. If an existing campaign is not working or it is considered "not successful," this process will reveal a clear diagnosis, which will help to improve it or provide justification for discontinuing it.

This book describes a credible, reliable process that can be used by organizations worldwide to measure the success of marketing projects and programs in a variety of industries and markets.

At first glance, the reader may wonder: *Is this just another book with another way to measure marketing results that is going to create a lot of work for me based mainly on assumptions?* As you go through the pages, it will quickly become clear that it is not. This book will transform the way professionals and organizations approach and think of marketing. Readers will soon see that the way we define "results" is not the same way many other books do. Audience, attendance, and visitors are *not* the results (output) generated by marketing but its input. The broadly used communication-only marketing model has died. Marketing, as much as logistics, finance, and human resources, is a business variable, and as such, general management and marketers overall should not fail to show its contribution to the business in an accountable way, such as cash flow and generated profit.

The ROI Marketing philosophy is the new way of putting marketing under the business umbrella. It is not about what you do, how you do it, or where you do it; it is about how it contributes to the communications *and* the business, showing its value in cash.

## Closing Points

- Marketing should be considered and treated as an investment rather than a cost.
- For all marketing projects, marketers should attempt to measure their contribution to the business in cash.
- Marketing goes beyond communicating a call to action with an ecologic and social-sustainability drive. It is about business sustainability as well.
- If it is not money, it is not ROI.
- ROI is the new marketing performance indicator standard.
- Measurement processes and procedures should be simple, robust, feasible, accurate, and reliable.

# Chapter II
# Measurement and Evaluation in Marketing

## Based on a True Story

Daniel Astley pressed the extension, "Mary, do you have five minutes? Can you come to my office please?"

Daniel was the marketing director of Electric Management Systems, a Chinese multinational company producing electricity components. Mary was the IT manager responsible for the CRM platform called "Future." I was in that meeting, trying to collect some missing pieces of information for the ROI Marketing Matrix prepared to determine the ROI in cash of ten events with potential clients around the country.

"Hi, Mary," said Daniel as she entered the room. "How can we know the quantity of sales opportunities that came from the events and how many of them turned into a sales transaction?"

"Let me open our dashboard to check it out…Here it is," said Mary.

On one screen shot, as a table, we had all client groups that went to the event on the top and a series of types of data on the left. Among these were leads, opportunities, and expected revenue from opportunities and won opportunities.

"This is new," said Daniel with pride. "We had this for the company worldwide only a couple of months ago. Now we can see all business-related information linked to what we do in marketing."

The meeting went on as I tried to dig into the data through questions:

"OK, it is clear to me where the leads come from, but what is an 'opportunity' for the system? Is there a request for a quote behind each opportunity?"

Mary jumped in. "An opportunity means that our salesperson considers that it might be worth it to explore the lead."

"Does this mean that there might be a request for a quote or not?" I asked.

"Not necessarily," she replied.

"And how do we know how many quotes have been done from leads coming from the events?" I insisted.

"We can't," she replied laconically.

"So, from opportunity we go to converted sales?" I asked.

"Not necessarily," she replied again. "A won opportunity doesn't mean that we have actually made the sale. It means that a client has said OK to a quote or proposal from us. But it does not register the actual sale."

I thought to myself, *If opportunities are not linked to a quote and won opportunities are not linked to actual sales, what is the value of this information?*

This was an actual dialogue from an actual client related to an actual situation that brought Albert Einstein to my mind: "Not everything that counts can be measured and not everything measurable counts."

## About Measuring ROI in Marketing

Measuring and evaluating results in marketing projects and campaigns has been and still is a hot topic at conferences and in webinars, articles, and business schools. It is also one of the most controversial and open-to-discussion issues among marketers and marketing forums. It is hard to find a common ground and a unified set of criteria that can help one to judge response, acquired knowledge, and call-to-action effectiveness (let alone efficiencies) in projects that have different media, different channels, a broad set of communication objectives, several KPIs, and a diffused link to business impact. Professionals and organizations struggle to find, use, and gain acceptance of ways to reliably measure and evaluate marketing projects. Furthermore, it is generally accepted, even by general management, that it is difficult to measure or evaluate marketing projects and campaigns from the business-impact point of view. Thus to the question "How much money did this campaign generate?" there is hardly an answer, and even worse, the question is never posed because most assume that it is not possible to measure it reliably.

Although interest in the topic has been heightened and much progress has been made—thanks in great part to access to new technologies and the advent of digital marketing—it is still an issue that challenges most marketing departments and pressures many general managers. But regardless of the position taken on the issue, the world economic turmoil, the change in consumer behavior, and the leveraging that digital marketing is offering to all advertisers, the claims for measuring and evaluating marketing are intensifying.

The dilemma surrounding the evaluation of marketing is a source of frustration for many senior executives even within the field itself. Most professionals realize that marketing investments are needed, but most of them struggle to find evidence to show them the actual accountable impact of marketing projects and campaigns on the business. Marketing becomes then an expense, one that is very easy to adjust, and is hardly considered as an investment. The return expected from marketing is connected to the results obtained in terms of the variables linked to the four pillars of marketing (product, price, placement, and communication), and although a certain degree of business impact can be inferred, in many cases, it is not quantified and mostly never accounted for. Moving up on the scale of value to really showing the money that marketing generates for the business is a daunting task, rarely achieved.

The trend in marketing evaluation goes toward measuring certain project inputs that, while showing value, fail to reveal cash flows needed for the business. This has lately been called "performance marketing." But while these inputs are part of the consequences of our marketing and are certainly a relevant set of data, they fail to show the direct influence of marketing on the business from the financial point of view. After all, marketing uses the financial resources of the company, why shouldn't it be measured against this resource? Marketers frequently face some of the following questions:

- How can I show the cash flows that marketing generates?
- How can I transform the results obtained in the communication/message level to the cash generated for the business?
- How can my measurement and evaluation gain credibility in the eyes of stakeholders?
- What if results are negative? What is the impact on my career? Is there any risk for me?

Unable to find clear and concrete responses to these questions, the industry shifted toward less-demanding measurable standards that became accepted but were far away from the expectations and needs for information of the C-level executives of advertisers. It is necessary to move from measuring reach and impact only to go further and deeper into business variables, especially profit.

This book shows how to measure the contribution of marketing in an accountable way. ROI is about money; it is the expected surplus of money generated after conducting a business practice. Measuring the ROI in marketing is the only way to show that marketing is an investment rather than an expense or a cost.

Based on this need for accountability, over the last several years, we've seen a trend of growing evaluation procedures, a trend that moves toward:

- measuring qualitative variables (online reputation, "likeability," positioning, etcetera)
- the use of digital tools, media, and channels to measure (social media, mobile devices, apps, etcetera)
- the use of new marketing tools and technology (geolocalization, new POS technologies, near-field communication, RFID (radio-frequency identification), etcetera)
- the search for new measurement standards (CTR, "likes," unique visitors, et cetera) replacing or broadening the traditional GRP and OTS.
- consumer involvement through the so-called "gained media," "social mention," "online reputation," etcetera

All of the above measure the inputs that the organizations' communication efforts generate, being those represented by the influence that marketing has on the way people think about their products and services, what they know about them, and what they do as part of the call to action (register "likes," visit the website, download the applications, talk about them on social media, et cetera). Few of them (if any) are really showing, by themselves, their impact on business variables, such as cash flow or profit. Furthermore, none of the above can show in a reliable and generally accepted way how much money it generated for the business, until now.

The use of ROI is emerging as an essential part of many measurement and evaluation systems. It is a fast-growing metric that most organizations have on their wish list. But only a few of them really measure ROI in marketing projects and almost none of them are ROI Marketing businesses.

What difference does it make whether we practice ROI or not?

| Marketing without ROI | Marketing with ROI |
|---|---|
| Activity-based | Results-oriented |
| Several KPIs for different projects | One KPI for all projects |
| Proven impact on communication only | Proven impact on communication and business |
| Marketing = cost or expense | Marketing = investment |

## What Is ROI Marketing?

ROI is a financial term used to define the value generated (return) by a given expenditure (the investment) once the expenditure has been discounted for. Its definition helps to guide future investment decisions, as it can determine future cash flows and opportunity costs of other investments. This works fine for all sorts of investments.

However, when financial staff members work out ROI calculations for any investments, they are generally capital goods expenditures of infrequent investments, with a long-term impact of usually large sums of money. Net present value (discounted future cash flows) is also usually included in the calculations. Marketing investments have a much different decision-making process and pattern. They are generally of a shorter-term horizon and cycle (usually one year or less), in many cases evaluating smaller amounts of money, and therefore, they occur with a much higher frequency. In addition, marketing projects and/or campaigns are scalable and have many different possible variations. This adds a new dimension to the concept of marginal investment and makes ROI evaluation and projection a much more relevant and impactful indicator. Marketers can do a €1 million advertising campaign or use the same creativity to do a €5 million campaign. They can use this amount of money to aim for the same goals but using a completely different set of media or channels. They can decide to invest this money in grassroots promotions for instance or a combination of campaigns. Furthermore, marketers can use the same type of media or channels to generate different outcomes. Financial and production personnel cannot use two completely different machines to produce the same product or decide to use the same machine to produce three different products with the same ease marketers could change either outcome or mean. This makes marketing investment decisions a much more complex process for which marketers and marketing as a discipline need a better way of gauging marketing's impact in order to increase credibility and raise the value of marketing within the organization.

This is what ROI Marketing is about. It implies changing the way marketers:

- o plan marketing,
- o execute marketing,
- o evaluate marketing results, and
- o report marketing results.

It does not mean revolutionizing the way we do marketing but evolving toward a more relevant, accountable, and impactful marketing. Working under the ROI Marketing philosophy entails:

- o a more relevant-to-the-business marketing strategy,
- o happy top executives with better decision-making capabilities,
- o improved bottom-line capabilities,
- o a better marketing budget negotiating position,
- o connecting and aligning the marketing department with the commercial/sales department,
- o better marketer professional skills, and
- o continuous improvement in marketing practices.

A simplified chain of marketing effects would show a picture like this:

Marketing projects planning => marketing delivery to the market => consumers' behavior => effect measurement

=> conclusions and assumptions => new projects planning

The ROI Marketing philosophy is adding a new dimension, contributing to the way marketers carry on the planning, execution, and measurement of marketing projects. It does not change the chain of marketing effects; it changes the way it evolves and the results it obtains. Practicing ROI Marketing means that marketing departments will move from planning based on past and future budget allocations to planning based on past and future returns.

## ROI Marketing Guidelines

As previously stated, no money, no ROI—and that holds true. Does this mean that by using the ROI Marketing Matrix companies will be able to measure the ROI of *all* projects and campaigns? Certainly not. There could be projects whose aim is not a clear accountable profit impact in the short term. Take for instance donations. We can establish a connection between how donations influence purchase decisions in a relevant, statistical way in order to infer the impact of that donation on sales for a given period. But the corporate team that originated the "idea" of donating may have done so not just to make a profit but also—and most important—to give society a clear message about the corporation's commitment to social or environmental sustainability. Through the donation, the company is talking to society about its values and principles. This, in the end, may influence purchasing decisions, but the aim of the donation is not such. The question then is: is it worth it to measure the ROI of this donation? Was obtaining a positive financial return on it one of its goals?

There might be other cases where evaluating the project from the ROI Marketing perspective would have an impact on the investment itself that is far too high (remember that the cost of measuring ROI is part of the marketing investment), making the evaluation unfeasible. In some of these cases, we can run an ROI Sensitivity Analysis and have a preinvestment check on the potential of a given project to deliver positive or negative returns.

One thing is certain, and that is that for both of the above-mentioned cases, we may not have an ROI figure at the end of the project. This does not mean that we cannot measure its impact on the ROI Marketing dimensions, such as impacts on the message, interactions, and costs. There should not be any blind investment hoping for some sort of intangible impact. Even if we collect the so-called "soft data," we can still measure impact. It is not financial, not an ROI, but still an impact. In many cases, this may be the aim of a project.

For all other projects aiming to have a positive impact on the bottom line of the business, the following *seven guidelines* will provide integrity to the overall process of evaluating and measuring.

## *ROI Marketing Guidelines*

1. Marketing efforts and plans should be *aligned* with the business's mission, vision, and global objectives.
2. It is not possible to measure the ROI of any project without previously setting the *right objectives*.
3. *Plan* to collect, analyze, and extract conclusions from data.
4. Analysts should use *significant data* (truly and consistently representing the group it relates to).
5. All data used should follow the most *conservative criteria*. Use the worst-case scenario.
6. To reach an ROI figure, it is necessary to use *financial* connections and measures (no money, no ROI).
7. *Validate* methodology with the reporting level prior to showing results. Build credibility and acceptance prior to showing results.

In all cases, readers should keep in mind that there is a certain possibility of measuring the ROI in all marketing projects. It is just a matter of time and resources.

## Barriers to Implementing ROI Marketing

Measuring the actual ROI of marketing (which we call a discipline/philosophy, "ROI Marketing") can be difficult and complex the first time, but with rigor and relevance, a good system of practices can be put into place in such a way that marketing does not suffer a revolution but an evolution toward becoming a more accountable and more impactful department. What are the main barriers that ROI Marketing faces in most organizations?

- *A clear definition of ROI in marketing*

How many times have we heard about ROI in marketing? How many times did we hear the same definition for such a simple acronym? I am sure the reader may have heard about performance marketing, ROI on emotions, return on credibility, and a long list of "returns" that somehow show the value (in most cases never monetary) generated by a marketing activity or project. But this variety of interpretations and lack of a clear definition is what is unwittingly hindering the credibility of the concept and marketing overall.

- *Lack of rigor and relevance*

As previously stated, ROI is a popular topic in many conferences, articles, events, and business schools. Lots of people are talking about it in various ways and using broad and light definitions. (I once read that in marketing, ROI equals ROA, returns on assets or that ROI in the events world is measured in "emotions" or experiences. Can you imagine your end-of-the-month payroll paid with *emotions*?) But worse yet, many methodologies or systems in place lack the systematic, conservative approach needed to make them credible.

- *The idea that measuring real ROI is too complex*

Evaluation can be difficult because projects are different, they use different media and channels, and industries and consumer segments vary vastly. Implementing an ROI evaluation process across multiple projects and/or campaigns could sometimes be quite complex. The challenge is to develop models that are theoretically sound, yet simple and usable. The overall idea is to build the measuring architecture starting from project/campaign planning in such a way that, during implementation, the methodology adapts to the project and not vice versa. In the end, ROI Marketing is a way of thinking and doing marketing. The first time, with no or limited processes in places and a lack of references, having to set up the measuring criteria and gaining internal momentum could become cumbersome. But soon, the efforts will pay off, and after the first cycle of practice, it will turn into a much more flawless and indisputably valuable procedure.

- *Lack of knowledge about how to link marketing inputs to outputs that have an impact on business*

The key to ROI Marketing is to be able to turn all marketing inputs into monetary outputs—meaning that with time, resources, and a sound methodology (like the ROI Marketing Matrix), marketers will be able to transform what they do on the communications level into money in all cases (including intangibles). For the purpose of linking results to business impact, it is necessary to know how to manage statistics, mathematical models, and business-related variables, such as net and gross profit margins, customer lifetime value, et cetera. The use of statistical models is confusing and difficult to absorb for most practitioners. Statistical precision is needed when high-impact/strategic variables are measured, but in many cases, simple statistics and calculations are all we need, and a sound system should already have those calculations embedded.

- *Evaluation is often taken as a post-project activity*

When evaluation is taken as an add-on process, it loses its capability to deliver measurable business results. Measurement and evaluation of marketing projects and campaigns should be blended as part of the very same project/campaign planning and architecture. It is from inception that objectives have to be defined; data collection planning and the whole project plan should be thought through from the ROI/business perspective as much as from the communication point of view.

- *Failure to see the medium/long-term payoff of evaluation*

When thinking about ROI Marketing, marketers should not be afraid of negative results; it would be much worse to have those negative results, not know about them, and keep losing money throughout the years. ROI marketing allows marketing departments to align with and show their contribution to the business objectives, linking such contribution to a budget (therefore transforming marketing into an investment). It also creates benchmarks for future projects, a solid support to those that work, and a clear picture of those that don't, making it easier to change processes and/or to eliminate them, contributing again to the business's health.

- *Lack of support from key stakeholders*

Important internal customers sometime fail to give the support needed to ensure the process's success.

Practicing ROI Marketing entails involving not only the communication tools and resources of the company but also all other departments that can become sources of information, stakeholders, and/or beneficiaries of the information. It is necessary to be able to count on executive or general management support to guarantee implementation success. ROI Marketing practices close the gap so often encountered between sales and marketing departments, bringing them closer and allowing them to work together with a common aim.

- *Uncertainty about the impact of measuring ROI at the personal level for the marketer*

Many marketing managers may ask, "But what happens if the ROI of my project is negative?" As previously said, management support to ROI Marketing is key to the process. If the organization is determined to consider marketing as an investment and to measure the financial return it generates, there is no doubt that regardless of the results, what is at stake is the contribution of the project to the business rather than the performance of the marketer. Clearly showing this contribution (whether negative or positive) can only speak well of marketers' professional skills and attitudes as members of the organization. Of course, if the results are negative, it is convenient (always thinking as a contributor to the employing company) to bring options and initiatives to turn these results into positive ones or to bring alternative projects that could or would have a positive return instead.

## Closing Points

- Marketing without ROI is a cost; with it, it is an investment.
- Plan and work to achieve business results through marketing rather than to execute its plans.
- The purpose, source, timing, and objectives of our measurements should be thoroughly thought through as part of the project-planning phase and prior to any execution.
- There is a planning phase and an execution phase on your way to ROI Marketing.
- Identify barriers and limitations; plan and work to overcome them.
- Identify enablers and leverage them along the process.
- Use technology with the aim to achieve results but also to collect data and measure.

# Chapter III
# The ROI Marketing Matrix: The Theory behind It

## Based on a True Story

It was September of 2009 and still warm in Barcelona. Anthony Gantt, the trade marketing director was again in charge of leading the overall project, one of the most visible ones after their massive advertising investments.

The participation of Dynamite, an isotonic drink, in the Anuga trade show in Germany was a classic. Anuga was one of the largest food trade shows in Europe, and as such, it congregated the most relevant and leading brands of the industry across all sectors. Dynamite was a historic participant to the trade show and had always had a very prominent space on the floor.

That morning in September, Tony, as everybody had called Anthony since he started to work as a temp in one of the factories twenty-five years earlier, had his first meeting with the committee to discuss the overall project for next year's participation. Yvonne, the French general manager, whom Tony had trained some fifteen years before, greeted him with a tepid kiss and sort of a distant hug (not that she lacked affection toward him, but she just didn't want to show it too much in front of the seven present members). The committee was composed of the GM, Yvonne; two board members; the VP of marketing, Paulo Telho (from Portugal); the purchasing director, Joanna Myers; the VP of sales, Martin Cerrutti; and me. I was an invited guest with a voice but no vote.

As we all sat down, Jerry McWire, one of the board members, opened up with a flat question: "Why do we have to go to this trade show? With all this crisis, shrinking sales and margins, and cost cuts, can we really afford to spend almost a million euro in going to a trade show to meet our clients that we will anyway meet regularly as usual?"

Paulo swiftly replied, "Because if we don't go, our clients are going to start thinking we are in a bad situation. Our reputation is at stake. If they think we are in a bad situation, they are going to start considering buying from somebody else. Even more, if our competitors see we are not going, they are going to be free to tell whatever story they want about our lack of participation, which could lead to who knows what…"

"Yeah, but our competitors are not spending as much as we are, and our clients may think that we are showing off while we could use the same money to give them discounts instead," said Martin.

"Although I must admit that our salespeople really use the show to get the chance to bond with their clients in a more relaxed, neutral environment, they also have the opportunity to gauge the market, what our competitors are showing firsthand, et cetera," he continued.

Joanne interjected, "All this is fine, but we need to cut down on our costs if we want to achieve our yearly profit goals, and this could be a great opportunity. Do we really need to spend this amount of money? Can we do it with a more contained budget, Tony?"

Tony was my friend, and he and I had already looked into different scenarios for this trade show. We knew the issue was not the amount of money spent but how and what they did prior, during, and after the trade show.

Even before Tony could answer, Jerry, the board member, jumped in again. "The question is not how much money we spend, but if we should spend it at all! What do we get out of these trade shows? I don't want to pay for parties or expensive dinners just to bond with our clients!"

**Introduction to the ROI Marketing Matrix**

Does this story ring a bell? Did you ever participate in these types of meetings? Maybe you can replace trade show with advertising, event, or sponsoring, but if you are a marketer, I doubt you've never faced a similar situation. Most marketing projects start with considerations close to the ones posed before.

That meeting went on. Tony and I had an ace up our sleeve. After a futile discussion about whether to participate or not based on "qualitative" reasons, Tony launched two questions:

1) How long could the impact of the trade show last on sales?

> 2) How much did they think was the impact of the trade show on the sales during that period?

The discussion went on for the next thirty minutes, and they finally agreed that the impact on sales could last three months and that it would not go beyond 2 to 3 percent of the sales of that period.

Tony and I had worked out our calculation through an ROI Sensitivity Analysis and determined the impact on sales during the following three months needed to recover the overall investment was 0.74 percent. Therefore, even if we halved the worst estimation of 2 to 1 percent, the trade show would still pay off. Suddenly, the discussion of whether we should go or not turned into how we could maximize profit in order to make money rather than just to pay it back. That was a magic moment in which we turned the point of view of the whole committee to considering the participation in the trade show as an investment rather than as a cost. Suddenly, ROI as a subject was on the table. But then came the challenging question: *But how are we going to measure it?*

The ROI Marketing Matrix has two defined phases to do so:

- the planning phase (ROI Marketing Cascade)
- the execution phase (ROI Marketing Ladder)

The planning phase deploys the ROI Marketing Cascade, which walks us through from business alignment to ROI validation of the project and/or campaign (ROI

Sensitivity Analysis). This is a necessary phase to ensure that once the marketing project has started, marketers not only work on the execution part of it but also on the measurement as part of the process and not as a post-project activity.

The execution phase is when marketing gets in contact with the market through the different touch points. With the ROI Marketing Ladder, we will work our way up by collecting data, relating the communications world to the business world, showing marketing's contribution in financial terms, and providing landmarks that will boost marketing into a continuous improvement process.

The ROI Marketing Matrix works under the assumption that if the goal is to determine the ROI of marketing projects and/or campaigns, everything that is measured in the first level of evaluation (communications) in any dimension (messages and/or interactions) should relate (cause-effect relationship) to the second level of evaluation (business) dimensions (cost and/or revenues) in a direct, unequivocal, and accepted way.

Figure 3.1. - ROI Marketing Matrix Evaluation Levels and Measurement Dimensions

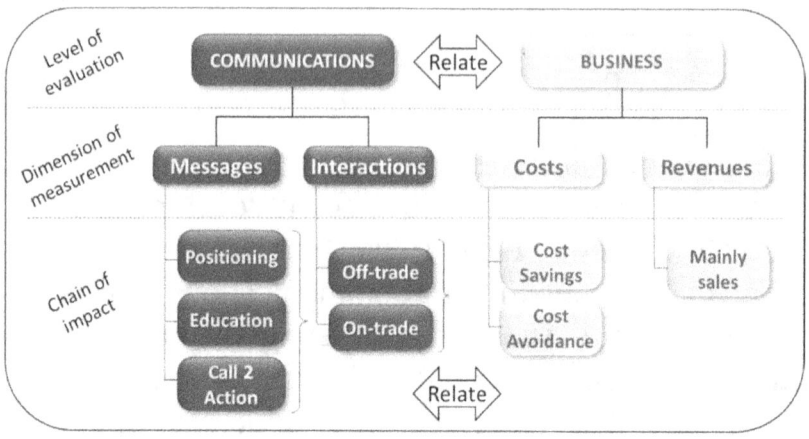

In order to demonstrate the financial impact of marketing, we need to establish a direct link between what we do and how it relates to the desired business outcome. For instance, if we want to increase sales, we should be able to show, in a reliable, credible, unequivocal, and accepted way, the relation between whatever KPI we are measuring for this purpose and the actual variation on sales. But this should never be the end of it. Do we know if this increase in sales is hurting or supporting the bottom line of the business? Furthermore, how can we establish and show the relation between marketing's contribution and the investment?

The ROI Marketing Matrix establishes objectives at the above-mentioned two levels (communications and business) and for all four dimensions of measurement (messages, interactions, costs, and revenues). Each of these measurement dimensions could also be broken down into subparts depending on the overall expected impact of the campaign or project.

What are the typical indicators (KPIs) that can help to define the objectives in each dimension? Marketing projects have a huge variety of typologies, from on- to off-line, below or above the line, integrated, on and off trade, in or out of home, et cetera. This diversity, which can sometimes add complexity to the ROI Marketing evaluation, can help the marketer to identify several performance indicators that will aid in defining the objectives, so they can plan the tactics and measure along the way.

The following table shows some of the most typical indicators used in marketing. The sources of relevant data that will demonstrate how these indicators will show performance are also vast. In marketing, in contact with the market, using the point-of-sale, digital media, and mobile technologies, it would be almost impossible to be unable to find ways to define indicators and collect relevant information about them.

| Level | Dimension | Subdimension | Common Performance Indicators |
|---|---|---|---|
| Communications | Messages | Positioning | o Awareness<br>o Reputation<br>o Target alignment |
| | | Education | o Degree of knowledge<br>o Demonstrated skills<br>o Degree of use |
| | | Call to Action | o Call to Action indicators are the |

| | | | |
|---|---|---|---|
| Business | Interactions | | actual interactions that the messages generate (see below) |
| | | Off-trade | o Attendance<br>o Online marketing<br>o Product test<br>o Direct marketing<br>o Advertising |
| | | On-trade | o Point-of-sale materials<br>o Promotions<br>o On-site registration<br>o Sampling<br>o Events |
| | Costs | Savings | o Marketing expenditures<br>o Etc. |
| | | Avoidance | o Tuition<br>o Fines<br>o Return rates |
| | Revenues | Generation | o Sales<br>o Customer lifetime value<br>o Distribution |

## Levels of Evaluation and Measurement Dimensions

1. Communications

The first level of evaluation is "communications." This refers to marketing as usual—the type everybody knows and which everybody in the company thinks he or she has the right to talk about. From the ROI marketing perspective, this level has two measurement dimensions:

1. *Messages*—Messages are delivered by all sorts of media, from conventional media (TV, press, and radio) to digital media and all other off-line media. In marketing, messages serve mainly three different purposes:

    a. *Positioning*—the place, image, or idea the consumer has about a given product and/or brand. It is linked to its price, channels of distribution, packaging, competition, brand image, etcetera.
    b. *Education*—everything the target group should know about accessing and/or acquiring the product: offers, where it is sold, new launches, availability of colors, etcetera.
    c. *Call to action*—this is a message that wants to persuade people to a conduct a given action (affiliation, registration, visit, etcetera). It is the main driver of the second measurement dimension.

2. *Interactions*—In marketing, this implies a given action the consumer is experiencing that may have an impact on communication objectives and may or may not have an impact on business objectives. Interactions happen in two different environments:

a. *Off-trade*—These are all those initiatives that happen outside of the point of sale. They are mostly related to bringing traffic to the point of sale, having a brand experience, and/or generating a first contact with the product or service. They could be on- or off-line and can also be carried on the company's own channels (website, social media, CRM, etcetera), gained (public relations, media coverage, etcetera), and purchased (search engine marketing (SEM), advergaming, advertising, etcetera) media.

b. *On-trade*—These are all those initiatives that happen within the point-of-sale environment. It is known that the biggest part of most purchasing decisions in fast-moving consumer goods consumption happens at the point of sale. That is why companies are more frequently making bigger efforts there.

The second level of evaluation is "*business.*" In this case, there is some hard data that unequivocally have an impact on business and can be measured in two dimensions:

1. *Costs*—costs can be of different types, ranging from cost savings to cost avoidance:

a. *Cost savings*—these include but are not limited to cost per acquisition (if segmentation is improved, for instance, the cost per acquisition will be reduced), presence at point of sale (the price of a preferred placement at the point of sale could be diminished if the marketing tactic plan includes, for instance, a benefit for the members of the point-of-sale loyalty program), improved churn rates, and diminished customer complaints, return rates, warranty claims, etcetera.
b. *Cost avoidance*—better procurement could lead to avoiding extra costs from suppliers; improved project planning can help to avoid fines and fees, etcetera.

2. *Revenues*—in this case, revenues indicate cash in-flows, which in most cases come from sales generated that can be attributed (in part or in whole) to the marketing action that is being undertaken.

## The ROI Marketing Cascade

As previously stated, every step mentioned in this part of the book belongs to the planning phase of our marketing plan in which we mention all necessary stages on our quest to find the financial return of marketing investments in summary, shown as the ROI Marketing Cascade.

Figure 3.2. - ROI Marketing Cascade ©

**About Business Alignment and Objectives**

If you carefully read the project briefs you receive from your clients (if you are working in an agency) or the ones written by yourself or your colleagues to the different agencies, you will notice that right from the start, briefings are mostly stating what to do. For instance: "We would like to do a direct marketing campaign," "a trade show booth," "an event," et cetera. During my more than twenty years of experience in an agency, I have always asked the question: "Why?" "Why do you want to do a trade show booth, an event, et cetera?" And most of the answers are usually the same: "Because we've been doing it for the last 'x' years, and it was very successful. I then immediately ask, "Why was it successful?" and I can sense how my interlocutor starts feeling a bit uncomfortable and, in some cases, even offended by me challenging his or her criteria of success.

The reason I ask this is that in theory, a briefing should clearly state the objectives and leave it to the professional service provider to propose the most efficient tool to achieve these objectives. Don't we do this when we buy media for instance? We do not say to the advertising or media agency, "I'd like this ad to be shown on CNN." Events, grassroots campaigns, consumer and/or point-of-sale activation, et cetera, are all means to reach a goal, not the purpose of marketing.

This is what "begin with the end in mind" means. Our project planning should focus on the objectives to reach rather than on the execution to achieve. I've never seen a brief stating, "We would like to make money with this project" or "We would like to achieve a positive ROI with this investment" or even "The project should pay for itself" as an objective.

Of course, many briefings have as an objective, at the end, "to increase sales." But is it really an objective stated this way, or is it a nice-to-have or, better yet, must-have objective that we know the boss wants to see in our plans?

This does not mean that marketers have to forget about marketing execution or don't have their say regarding what could work best to achieve their objectives. After all, marketers are the ones who have the experience with the brand, the products, the services, and the touch points with the target groups and markets. But if we want to measure the ROI of our marketing projects and/or campaigns during their planning, we should consider all the variables we've been thinking of to date but also all those that will help us to evaluate the project from a financial perspective as well, impacting the business's bottom line.

And here we get into the second point: marketers must not lose sight of the objectives in the four dimensions of evaluation. A good ROI Marketing practitioner will always see the twofold world marketing impacts on: the world of messages and interactions (called, in the ROI Marketing Matrix, the communications level) and the world of finance (business level).

As we said at the beginning, the ROI Marketing Matrix establishes two levels of evaluation (communication and business), each of which contains two dimensions of measurement (messages and interactions and costs and revenues). Whatever we do at the project and/or campaign level should and will have an impact on each and every one of these levels. The questions the ROI Marketing Matrix answers are whether we know it or not and how we are going to demonstrate it.

The communications level of evaluation is about our marketing as usual. We move in this level in our day-to-day work. We and our marketing agencies think about messages that aim to generate a positioning in the mind of customers and/or to teach something to our consumer segments, and, in many cases, we establish interactions (participation, registration, redemption, sampling, tests, et cetera) that ultimately lead to an increase in sales. But this doesn't mean that the contribution of marketing to the business is positive, even if we somehow manage to relate a certain increase in sales to our marketing project or campaign.

As comedian Groucho Marx would say, "If you don't know where you go, you may end up anywhere." The way we define where we want to go in marketing is through alignment with the business mission, vision, and strategy through a set of objectives for each and every project.

The marketing strategy should be in clear and evident arrangement to whatever the business stakeholders have decided are their objectives and the purpose of the enterprise overall. This means that we should see marketing from a more holistic approach in its accordance with and impact on the overall vision and mission of the business, its objectives, and its strategy. It calls for an overall integrated strategy approach that goes beyond (and before) whatever we do as a marketing activity and regardless of the channel or media. This overall business alignment should reign and show in the marketing plan. It should be present in all day-to-day ad hoc work and in the touch points that every member of the organization will use internally, with suppliers, and with clients and consumers.

Each marketing department should have a clear set of principles that will help them to assess whether whatever they are doing is "aligned" or "not aligned" with the business. The KPIs that we establish in our marketing plan should also show the impact of marketing on those values. A profitable marketing plan (positive ROI) would be of little help if it is not building around the corporation's guiding principles and scope in such a way that it establishes a symbiotic relationship with them.

In this ever-changing market, with rapid movements in consumer behavior, it is imperative that regardless of their marketing tactical implementation, marketers have an overall vision of what they do in regards to what it means to the business. The whole world of marketing is changing. The messages we used to deliver through conventional media (TV, press, and radio) are moving to their digital version. Their digital version is being transformed by the way they interact with social media, and social media is more and more often accessed on mobile devices by consumers on the move. It is harder and harder to predict what consumers will do and the way they will influence marketing plans. The consistency of companies' marketing plans with their philosophies, scopes, missions, and visions, regardless of media, channel, or marketing activity carried, is of the essence to establish a clear, durable, and positive relationship with audiences and markets, wherever they are and however they communicate.

If our marketing strategy is aligned with the business, the next step is to make sure we have the right marketing strategy, and that begins with setting the right objectives.

Objectives should be clearly stated, be achievable, and above all, be measurable. Most of the time, objectives are defined as a set of intentions that in many cases are proved by results that are inferred from project inputs. For instance, if the objective was that we should increase awareness about our new product, we inferred that by having "x" amount of unique visitors to our website, we managed to develop such awareness. But is this the right conclusion to draw? Shouldn't we verify, somehow, that such awareness was certainly developed?

In the ROI Marketing Matrix, we should set objectives for every project and on each of the two levels of evaluation: communications and business. Within these levels, we should also establish goals for each one of the four measurement dimensions: messages, interactions, costs, and revenues. Finally, if measurement processes have already been used in the past or if we have a clear, usable, and accepted reference, we may or even should set ROI objectives for each and every marketing project or campaign.

Many people believe that measuring ROI in marketing is not possible, but remember, as the philosopher Ernst Cassirer would say: "We can hardly blame science just because we've asked the wrong questions." Without clear, measurable objectives, there's no way we can start our quest for marketing accountability and everything that such accountability entails.

During the objective-setting process, we should consider not only their impact on the communication and finances of the business (the two evaluation levels), but also their complete alignment with the business. If our company, for instance, is standing for the three dimensions of sustainability (social, environmental, and economic), our marketing objectives should clearly aim to satisfy that philosophy and view as well.

Objectives are the cornerstone of the marketing plan and will set the different projects that will be part of the various campaigns. Project planning is then the starting point on the road to delivery and success, and as such, it should be very well thought through.

It is common to see communications (understanding communications as messages delivered with the aim to position and/or teach and/or as a call to action) objectives in all or most marketing projects or campaign briefings, including awareness, reach, impressions, impact, intentions, affiliation, et cetera. While these objectives are valid and certainly necessary as part of the nature of marketing, they are not comprehensive of the overall potential that marketing could have in the business. What characteristics should marketing objectives have if they want to be business driven?

## Requirements of Objectives

Objectives must be:

- *Measurable and quantifiable*
  All objectives should be measureable and quantifiable. This is a condition sometimes not met even in communications objectives. What are the variables that we should be measuring to have an impact on business? Of course, this is in the basics of business alignment; these variables could be financial measures, such as costs, revenues, and profits, or they could be variables that are related to the core and scope of the business (such as $CO_2$ footprint, social impact, et cetera).

- *Time-framed*
  All objectives should have a measurement-final milestone. In the case of ROI Marketing, this milestone is set by the length of time we consider our project may have impact on. For instance, if measuring the impact of a trade show booth in the corporate communications and business, how long does the marketer think the trade show is going to have an impact on them? In other words, how long is the influence of the trade show going to last? It is advisable that this period of time is agreed to by the main stakeholders or evaluating body so it is acceptable from the very beginning.

- *Achievable*
  
  It may seem like common sense, but frequently, managers overlook this sine qua non characteristic of any objective. Achievability (or lack thereof) will become evident during project or campaign planning and be completely confirmed with the ROI Sensitivity Analysis (developed at the end of this chapter), which should be carried out prior to the execution phase. Later in the book, we will look at an example of a real project, which even before investing the first euro, we already knew was going to lose money for sure, and how the client failed to see it.

*An objective without a plan is a dream.*

## About Project Planning

Once our marketing strategy has been established, our marketing objectives set, and our marketing tactics defined, we are ready to embark on the quest toward project planning. Project planning from the ROI Marketing perspective is not much different from what marketers are used to doing generally. It just requires a broader perspective and an understanding that the reach of the activities to be carried out go beyond what was usually thought of as the scope of marketing and that it will go all the way to the bottom line of the business. What are the main requirements of project planning within the ROI Marketing Matrix?

- It should *focus on delivery* rather than on execution. Begin with the end in mind.
- *Never lose sight of the objectives* that drive the plan in all four dimensions of evaluation (messages, interactions, costs, and revenues). Always ask: how is this task / activity / action / event / advertising / direct marketing / et cetera going to contribute to achieving any of the different objectives?
- Plan how you are going to *establish a cause-effect relation* between what you achieve from marketing and the business objective at stake. *Validate* that relation with the person you are reporting to. Is it acceptable / reliable / believable?
- Think about how you are going to *collect specific information* about the KPIs that will demonstrate that you have achieved the objectives. This is where you should make the what, when, who, and how checklist (3WH checklist).
- Plan also on which basis you are going to *give a monetary value* to each of the KPIs measured. *Validate* such criteria with the person you are reporting to. Is it acceptable / reliable / believable?
- Start defining and controlling the *costs involved and impacted* (marketing expenditures and influence on current costs).
- *Validate* before execution (ROI Sensitivity Analysis). What are the chances this project and/or campaign might be successful?

## Does My Project Make Sense from an ROI perspective? ROI Sensitivity Analysis

It would not be a sound strategy not to validate our plan from the ROI perspective. This is what is called the ROI Sensitivity Analysis.

The ROI Sensitivity Analysis is a process by which we will determine, prior to investing, whether the project we are about to start could make or lose money. It consists of matching business objectives and the allocated budget to the impact needed to achieve those objectives. It is not an exact measure to begin with, but it starts building ROI awareness around marketing, showing that we are not only concerned with the "soft" results but also the hard, accountable data. And, most important, the validation with the commercial and sales division will begin to build support for ROI Marketing around the project prior to starting it. The ROI Sensitivity Analysis consists of finding the financial break-even point of any project and then considering, in a relevant and statistically rigorous way, the chances of achieving that break-even point with the planned investment and objectives. Let's look at it with a real example (type of product, names, brands, and regions are fictional):

Company: Household & Toiletries Leader in South America
Brand: Freshen-up Shampoo
Investment: $100,000
Points of sale: 5,000

Objective: To increase marginal sales in hypermarkets of five countries by any percentage in a two-month period from April to May.

Mechanic: POS (point of sale) activation through a giveaway linked to the purchase of the second unit of the product.

Product in promotion per display: 50 units per POS per month

Gross margin per product sold: $0.60/unit

Purchase cycle: once a month

Total sales in units in two months: 2,000,000 units

With all this information, we should be able to know, again prior to investing, whether this marketing project makes sense or not from the ROI perspective. How do we do it? It is quite simple in this case. (By the way, this particular client failed to do this analysis.)

Maximum marginal sales expected:
25 units x 5,000 POS x 1 month = 125,000*
Impact on overall sales: 125,000/2,000,000 = 6.25%
Maximum possible profit by project: $0.60 x 125,000 = $75,000
Break-even point units needed: 166,667 units

*If our project aims to increase marginal sales through the purchase of the second unit, we are taking 50 percent of the display in advance (thus 25 units as 50 percent of the 50 units per POS) and increasing the speed of the purchase cycle but losing the sale of the second month (that's why we multiply by only one month even though

the second month a new set of customers could be stocking for two months).

Conclusion: In this case, we do not need to ask anybody. It is clear that even if we sell 100 percent of the units in the promotion, we will lose $25,000 ($100,000 investment - $75,000 maximum possible profit).

Now, for the sake of the example, imagine that the margin was $1. This would bring the maximum possible profit to $125,000 (a possible ROI of 25 percent), meaning that the break-even point is below the maximum possible profit. We should then ask if it is feasible/credible to reach a 6.25 percent impact on sales per month. The way to do this is by asking our own sales force and, if possible, the very same points of sale. After all, they are the ones who are on the front line and know by heart how much a given campaign can impact sales in any given period based on experience and observation.

But the opinion of a few won't necessary be right; therefore, we need to ask a statistically relevant sample of people who can give us a low margin of error (ideally 5 percent or lower) with as a high a confidence level (ideally 95 percent or above) as possible. Let's work that out.

In this case, the company did not have a close relationship with the points of sale, so it was not possible to ask them. Let's assume then that we use our own sales force as the best gauge of our project efficacy. We are going to ask what influence, based on their experience and observation, a direct giveaway for a second purchased unit could have on the purchase decision at the point of sale.

The sales force of Freshen-up Shampoo was 350 people. A representative sample that has a 5 percent margin of error and a 95 percent level of confidence is 183 people. This means that we need to ask at least 183 people. This is a mathematical calculation; if you are not familiar with the arithmetic for statistics, you can find dozens of websites and apps that can do this for you in a few seconds. Just look for setting a sample size or "sample-size calculator." Let's assume that we ask (in the real case, we never reached this point, as the client refused to do the Sensitivity Analysis) and the answer we achieve has a result of 8 percent for the sake of the example. Eight percent is higher than the 6.25 percent that we calculated previously. Should we take this percentage as such and assume then that this project will have a positive ROI? We should not. As we want the whole process to be reliable, credible, and acceptable, we need to be more rigorous in analyzing the data, and we should correct this percentage by the margin of error and the level of confidence. To be conservative, if we said that the sample has a 5 percent margin of error, we should then subtract that from the achieved figure: 8 percent then becomes 7.68 percent, but we should also multiply this again for the confidence level. Then it becomes 7.3 percent. As we see, this corrected level is very close to the 6.25 percent needed to break even, so further careful measurement and analysis should take place if we really want to determine whether this could be a money-making project or not.

Maybe this small of a difference between appreciated project impact and the break-even point might call for some adjustments. For instance, we could reduce the investment or downgrade the objective to accept some losses in exchange for the learning process of measuring the ROI for the first time or considering the fact that stocking the product should also hinder competitors and diminish their market share during the second month or the fact that by having a giveaway present at home, consumers will have a greater brand awareness, which will drive future purchase decisions increasing the customer lifetime value and thus the returns in the longer run.

But what happens if we do the ROI Sensitivity Analysis and the results of the validation are negative?

The ROI Sensitivity Analysis serves several purposes:

- o to know or have an idea beforehand whether the project will/could make or lose money
- o to minimize the risk of the investment.
- o to take preventive actions in case of dark clouds on the horizon
- o to increase ROI Marketing awareness and support within the organization
- o to improve the chances of a positive financial return on marketing investments

So if up front, the results don't look very good or are too close to losing money for comfort, we can take several actions:

Figure 3.3. _ ROI Sensitivity Analysis Scenarios and Actions

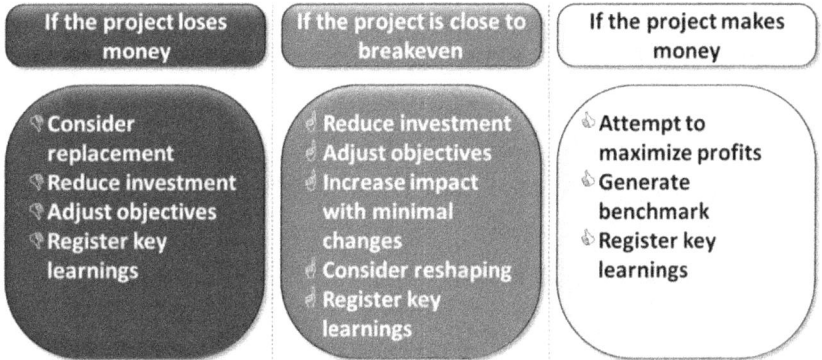

Remember, when a project loses money, the fact that we or the organization don't know about it doesn't mean that the project stops generating losses. Sooner or later, the consequences of inaction will take a toll.

The above-mentioned actions are all project related, but the reader may rightly question also what the impact on his/her position in the company will be. Identifying a money-losing project (even if it is a "classic" project within the company, like a trade show booth, for instance) doesn't really have a negative impact on the job of any person. It can only speak well about his/her professional skills, analytical competence, ability to think and look beyond the boundaries, and business alignment capabilities. Therefore, a marketer should never be afraid to bring up the subject if a project does not look so good from the financial point of view. After all, when analyzing a project or campaign, we are not evaluating the professional performance of a person but the project and/or campaign contribution to communications *and* to the business.

However, and especially if it is one of those projects that is well established within the company and is seen as one of those "things" that cannot be moved, it is always advisable to incorporate within our analysis an alternative project, campaign, or use of the budget. This way, we are treating marketing money as an investment portfolio and building around marketing rather than hindering it.

Everything mentioned so far refers to and happens within the planning phase of the ROI Marketing Matrix implementation. We have not invested resources other than our time and its opportunity cost (which in this case, considering the stakes, should not be so high).

Once the ROI Marketing Cascade has been worked through, it is time to take action. This second phase is achieved with the ROI Marketing Ladder, which translates the planning into actions and steps that should be incorporated into the usual project-execution process and implementation.

## Putting It All Together—The ROI Marketing Ladder

Once the ROI Sensitivity Analysis has been completed and conclusions have been drawn regarding whether the project should be developed or not, it is time to take action. Actions after the ROI Sensitivity Analysis could take one of two directions:

1. If the results are not satisfactory, modify the objectives, the plan, or the budget (separately or together) to make them satisfactory.
2. If the results are satisfactory, start with the project execution or implementation.

This last stage is the kickoff of the second phase: the execution phase. During the execution phase, marketers should put into practice everything as it was planned during the planning phase—not just the project activities, such as delivering the mail, publishing the media, carrying the event, et cetera, but also gathering all the data they planned to collect, relating communication impact to business impact, converting impact into money, and calculating the ROI of the marketing project and/or campaign to be able to extract conclusions for future marketing investments.

All these steps give shape to the ROI Marketing Ladder (see next page).

Figure 3.4. – ROI Marketing Ladder

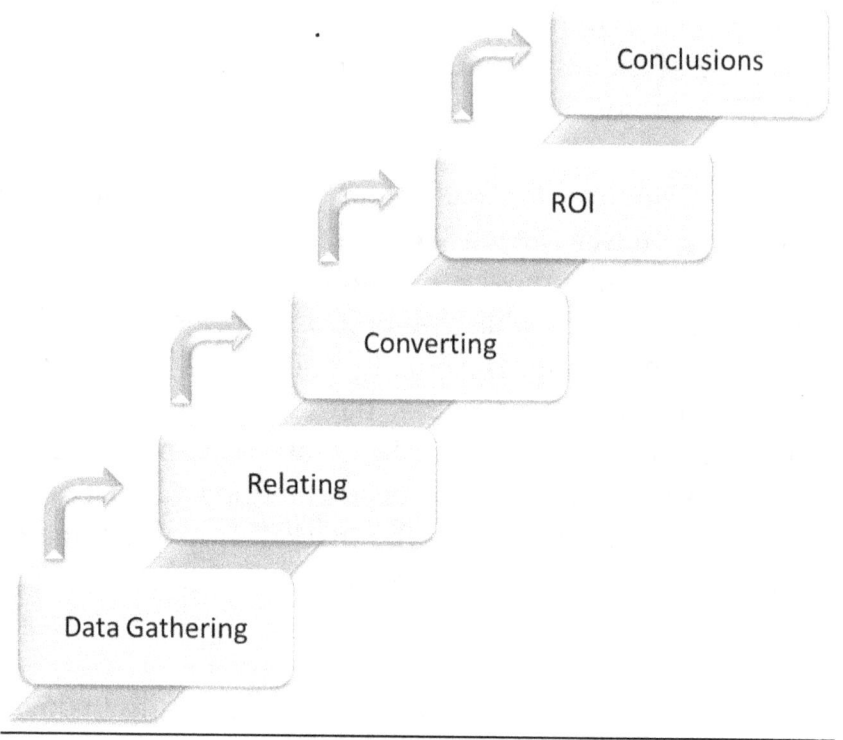

This book will walk you through all these steps in a detailed manner in part 2 so you can take ROI Marketing from theory to practice.

By implementing the ROI Marketing Matrix, marketers should be able to start viewing marketing (and lead the whole organization to do so) from a different perspective, bringing it up to the business level and, above all, making it accountable from a financial point of view. After the first cycle of evaluations (either for a project or for a whole year campaign), marketers will be able to start making decisions with a completely new set of tools, which will allow them to treat marketing projects as an investment. Since projects will have different measured and expected results, marketing departments will be able to see them as an investment portfolio and make decisions based not only on the communications needs of the company but also on its business strategy in total alignment.

The ROI Marketing Matrix will also give marketers the opportunity to negotiate the coming year's budget from a totally different position. Marketing directors will not be "asking" for money to execute their plan but rather deploying an investment portfolio that will bring profit to the business through marketing. Diminishing budgets will stop taking the shape of "cuts" since executives can only cut costs. If we are able to show the contribution of marketing to the bottom line with the profitability of marketing projects, any decision about decreasing a budget will be about giving up on the profits that that given project was expected to generate. A general manager deciding not to invest resources in something that has a traceable profitability will have to explain to shareholders the alternative use of those resources, as there will be a clear and accountable opportunity cost.

Summarizing, the ROI marketing Matrix has two defined phases: the planning phase (the framework of which is represented by the ROI Marketing Cascade) and the execution phase (the framework of which is represented by the ROI Marketing Ladder). During the planning phase, marketers should work step by step through business alignment, setting up the right objectives to define a proper marketing strategy. This will translate into a marketing plan that will not only focus on the execution of the marketing activities that will bring the expected results but also on measuring with communication and business (financial) aims. Closing the planning phase is the ROI Sensitivity Analysis to sense, prior to investing, the likelihood of the project achieving a positive or negative return, its feasibility, and the alignment between the objectives and investment.

At kickoff during the execution phase, marketers will collect data in a rigorous and relevant way to create correlations between how marketing and communication variables impact on business variables. They will then convert those impacts into monetary values and calculate the return generated by the marketing investment. Finally, the whole process would be only halfway complete if conclusions were not drawn and deeper analyses were not conducted. The overall idea of the ROI Marketing philosophy is that marketing departments can not only measure the ROI of executed projects but also use these results to make better decisions on future projects and campaigns. The methodological framework of the ROI Marketing Matrix looks like this then (see next page):

## Figure 3.5. - ROI Marketing Matrix Methodological Framework

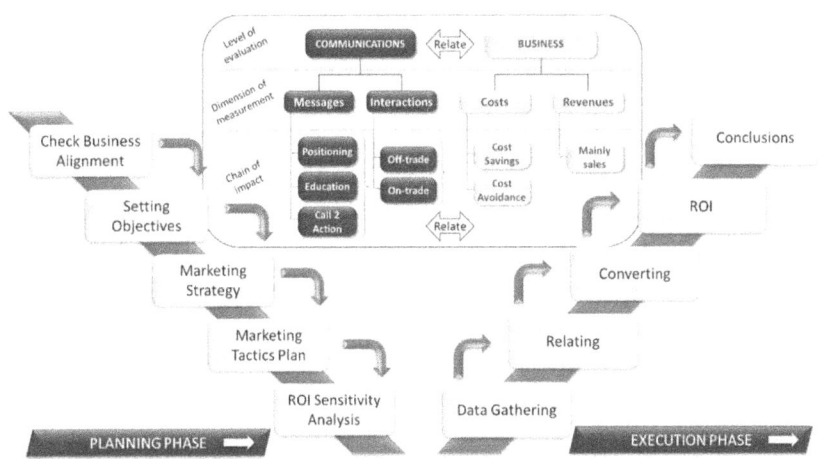

Within this framework, the ROI Marketing Matrix defines a step-by-step process that drives execution toward the accountability of marketing tactics to implement.

## About Data Collection

"Forty-two percent of marketing data comes from external sources, including social networks…"
—Highlights from Gartner's *Data-Driven Marketing Survey*, 2013

Needless to say, all the KPIs mentioned in this book come as a reflection of something that happens in the real world and therefore, when it comes to data, marketers should: *define the data, plan and collect the data, and analyze the data.*

Since we need to collect data before, during, and after the execution of our marketing projects or campaigns, in order to generate cause-effect relationships that will show the contribution of marketing to the communications of the corporation and to its business (bottom line), we should plan how to define all the information necessary to demonstrate those relations, and here is where the "3WH checklist" comes in handy (table 3.1). The data should be relevant and collected with a methodology that guarantees that it is accurate and true to the best extent and that can safely demonstrate that it was collected during the pre-established period for the evaluation process.

Table 3.1. - 3WH Checklist

| | |
|---|---|
| **What** | What is the information I need to collect? What type of data? This represents the KPI that shows the variation on each dimension of measurement. For instance, which is the indicator that will show whether I reduced my costs or not? |
| **When** | When is the information going to be retrieved? When is the right moment to obtain the answers to a questionnaire? For instance, make sure that if you ask a question related to the contents of a congress, you request the questionnaires after the congress is over and not before. |
| **Who** | Who owns the information? Whom should I ask for it? Sometimes we fail to obtain necessary information just because we are |

|  | looking for it in the wrong place. For instance, who knows best about preference in medicines of patients, doctors or pharmacists? |
| --- | --- |
| **How** | How am I going to collect the above-mentioned piece of information? Is it going to be done on a survey? By counting people? Through a questionnaire? It represents the method needed to collect the data. For instance, can I obtain levels of sales from my own organization, or should I get it from the distribution? |

*Types of Data to Collect*

There are three sets of data to collect:
1. data related to the performance of our communications efforts (messages and interactions)
2. costs of marketing and costs affected by the project (for saving and avoiding purposes)
3. revenues generated by the marketing project

1. Performance Data

This is probably the easiest of all the sets of data, as it is the one marketers and agencies are used to working with. It refers to all indicators that show the impact of messages (awareness, positioning, intention to purchase, knowledge, et cetera) and interactions (attendance, traffic, impact, impressions, visits, affiliation, et cetera). It will never be seen as money.

To collect this type of data, marketers can use:
- market studies
- focus groups
- digital tools
- surveys and questionnaires
- industry associations reports
- Own measurements
- R&D reports
- benchmarking data
- simple counting (attendees, registrations, visits, et cetera)
- and so on

2. Costs Data

The only way we will be able to calculate the return on marketing investments is by comparing the business results to the investments (marketing expenditures) made to achieve those results. Therefore, a strict control and definition of costs (the second set of data to collect) is necessary to achieve a reliable ROI figure. The data referring to costs will come from the very same organization and its procurement system most of the time. Costs are therefore a different set of data, but this does not mean that we should not keep the same level of rigor and relevance criteria. What are the costs or types of costs that we should consider to determine the ROI of a marketing project and/or campaign? The following list is not exhaustive, but it certainly covers the most common marketing-related direct costs:

- ✓ cost of media buy

- ✓ cost of own media (campaign microsite, community management, etcetera)
- ✓ cost of project implementation (booths, direct marketing, point-of-sale material, catering, venue fees, events, etcetera)
- ✓ giveaways
- ✓ personnel directly hired for the project and/or campaign
- ✓ other project tuitions like legal consultation, insurance, agency fees, etcetera

Most of these costs are controlled and handled by the marketing department itself. To gather them, it may also require the participation of other departments (internal or external—outsourced). It will only show as money and will refer to all the direct costs of marketing plan implementation. Remember, it is only the direct costs of a project or campaign as most nonproject-related marketing costs (such as marketing personnel, R&D, et cetera) are embedded in the cost of goods sold (COGS).

To collect this type of data, marketers can use:
- o own records
- o procurement department reports
- o corporate financial reports
- o internal consultation
- o industry associations reports
- o benchmarking data
- o control of own expenditures
- o et cetera

What are the costs that we should *not* consider for ROI purposes?

- ✓ company marketing personnel—Although they will be investing their time on the project, the allocation of this cost is already embedded in the gross margin of the product, so it should not be accounted for.
- ✓ opportunity costs—Even though they exist (for the opportunity cost of the time used as much as for the opportunity cost of the money invested), validating this amount would be a daunting task that goes beyond the scope of the evaluation. However, once the first round of ROI evaluation is done for a repetitive type of project, it may be possible to gauge the opportunity cost of a new project compared to a relevant marketing investment already gauged.
- ✓ new product development—If it is already embedded in the cost of goods sold and therefore is reflected in the gross margin.
- ✓ new packaging development (unless we are evaluating the ROI of the new packaging as a marketing project)
- ✓ distribution costs—It is already embedded in the cost of goods sold and is therefore reflected in the gross margin.

There is a second set of costs that marketers should consider, and those are the ones that are affected by the marketing project and not held because of it. If, as a consequence of the marketing project, for instance, consumers start using a product in a different way that reduces breakage and warranty claims, this reduction in claims will imply fewer costs that will go directly to the bottom line of the business. This cost avoidance will also affect the ROI of the project and should be accounted for.

If we want to obtain the return on marketing investments, we need to go all the way to the end, meaning that we need to be able to convert all variables in all dimensions at all levels into money. This is not an easy task, especially if we are doing it for the first time and are lacking a past reference. However, no money, no ROI. We can always settle for less, stay at the communications level (as it is commonly done), and show the results of a campaign in terms of its impact on awareness, purchase intentions, impressions, et cetera. In some cases, it will depend on the cost of measuring and its impact on the overall project. For instance, if measuring the ROI of a single marketing project costs between €5,000 and €10,000, is it feasible to measure the ROI of a point-of-sale activation project that costs €15,000? Most likely not, as measuring the ROI could outweigh the project's budget itself. However, in this particular case, since we are talking about a point of sale, if we managed to obtain the sell-out of that given point and compare it to another under the same conditions that did not have the project's impact (control group), or the same one during the same period of another year without the project, we might be able to reach the acceptable conclusion, keeping all other factors the same, that the project is responsible for the difference in sales between those stores. If there is a will, there is a way.

3. Revenues Data

At this stage, we reach a critical point in measuring the ROI of marketing investments, and that is relating the effects (communications results) to monetary outcomes (business results). But before that, let's try to bring some light to the subject (see table 3.2)

Table 3.2. Communications Results Versus Business Results

| Communications Results | Business Results |
|---|---|
| Event attendance | Act of purchase |
| Unique visitors to a website | Cost reduction |
| Intention to purchase | Cost avoidance |
| CTR (Click-through ratio) | Loyalty variations |
| "Likes" | Cross-selling |
| Social mention | Up-selling |
| Recruitment | Client retention |
| MGM (member gets member) | CGC (client gets client) |
| Leads | Distribution variations |
| Estimates | Improve listing |
| Redemption when is not linked to sales | Redemption when linked to the act of sale |
| Etcetera | Etcetera |

Revenues data are more complicated but still feasible to obtain, as it is necessary to establish the link between what marketers do and the money that these actions generate for the business. In this sense, it is necessary to define how each one of the performance indicators is going to be converted into money. In some cases, when there is a clear cause-effect relation (redemption, for instance), it will be clear and indisputable. Still, there will be many cases in which this relationship is not direct and in these cases, marketers will have to work assumptions, statistics, and validation procedures in order to guarantee acceptability, reliability, and robustness of the data.

To collect this type of data marketers can use:

- sell-out records (own or from distribution)
- sell-out estimations based on sell-in
- historical conversion records
- customer lifetime value
- industry associations reports
- benchmarking data
- etcetera

As long as we are not able to translate any of the results coming from projects into money for the business, the impact of our marketing will stay within the "communications level." This means that we do not have an ROI figure and marketing will be considered a cost rather than an investment or will be optimistically seen as an investment on which returns cannot be measured or seen in quantity or time.

That is why conversion ratios are so important and should be part of our project planning. We should try to convert all communications results into business results by relating their impact on business variables and establishing a criterion to convert them into monetary values. This way, we start with an inflow of money into marketing and finish with an outflow of the same kind: money. But how can we find or generate these conversion ratios in marketing? In the answer to this question lies the basics for the collection of the third set of data: revenues.

## Translating Communications Results into Business Variables

### *About Conversion Ratios*

The fact that we have worked out the sales revenue generated by a project or campaign doesn't mean that our project is a sustainable one from a financial point of view. Are we making money with it?

Without conversion ratios, it would be difficult, if possible at all, to calculate the returns of marketing investments. There are two main steps needed to reach such a ratio: relating and converting.

*Relating*:

Relating refers to finding the cause-effect relation between the inputs generated by the messages and interactions (communication level) and their impact on the costs and revenues (business level). This relation has to be unequivocal to the best extent. This means that analysts should base their calculations on certain correlations and/or on accepted estimations. There are several possible ways in which marketers can generate these correlations when planning to build them in advance. That is why planning to measure ROI is so important, as it will most likely not be possible to establish these cause-effect relations as a postexecution activity.

Some of the ways to build cause-effect relations include:

- control groups
- Multiple regression
- questionnaires and surveys
- corporations' own records
- Cluster analysis
- Multi-attribute compositional models (conjoint analysis)
- trend line analysis
- etcetera

The more direct the correlations, the more reliable and accepted they are. For instance, if the project evaluator can have a direct measure of the whole population (in the case of a niche market, business to business for instance), there will be no questioning regarding the accuracy and significance. As the direct link fades through population size, the relevance of data starts to weaken. If no direct measure of the full population is available, then a controlled test could give an accurate and acceptable level of reliability. It is always a good practice to validate such acceptability prior to using it. When no direct measurement is possible (either of the full population or through a control group), premeasured standards and/or benchmarks can give a valid correlation between marketing activities and business impact. Last, if no premeasured standards or benchmarks are available (either internally or externally), key stakeholders' assumptions can also be considered. Key stakeholders could include the company's own sales force, distribution channels, point-of-sale information (sell-out for instance), industry associations, consumers, et cetera. Relating can also be achieved through a technique called trend line analysis that can establish a cause-effect relation through population or variable behavior before and after the implementation of a project.

The following figure shows some of the methods of converting communications results into business results with their degree of indisputability. It is obvious that the stronger the link between the cause of the input and its impact (effect) on the business, the more indisputable the data will be.

Figure 3.6. - Relating Effects and Indisputability of Data

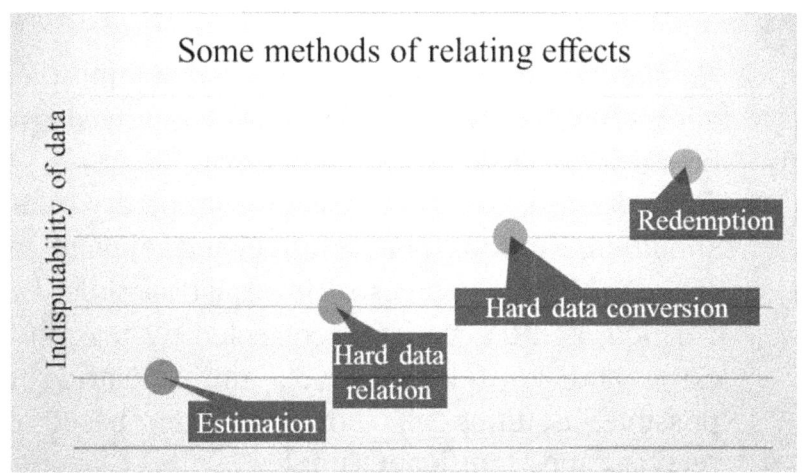

*Converting*:

Once we have established a relationship between the two levels of evaluation (communications and business) and determined the impact of the first one over the second one, it is necessary to value these impacts in terms of money. Remember: no money, no ROI.

As previously mentioned, the only way we will be able to connect the marketing to the business is through conversion ratios. Ultimately, we will be able to transform marketing performance into business performance. In other words, during the planning phase of our project or campaign, we will set diverse criteria to convert all the variables we formerly saw on table 3.2 (page 86) as communications results into monetary outcomes (business results).

These criteria to relate communications to business must follow a standard:

- *Be simple*: everybody should understand them across functions (CEO, CFO, CMO, purchasing, et cetera).
- *Be robust*: the way it assigns monetary value should be rigorous, conservative, and relevant.
- *Be reliable*: the sources of information should be verified, and the statistics corrected by margin of error and confidence level; the scenarios or possible assumptions should also be based on relevant and significant samples.
- *Be accepted*: if it is not previously accepted, chances are that during the report presentation, marketers will end up discussing the methodology rather than the results of the project or campaign.

But how do we do it? For instance, let's assume that we are doing a digital campaign that includes SEM (search engine marketing, where we pay per each click to whatever link (landing page) we create in the advertising on specially segmented searches) and a very active social media group where we want our consumers to interact and talk about our product or brand.

What are the communications results? Clicks, visits to the social media group, and "likes," for instance. And so far, this is business as usual. But I don't think any of us would accept Facebook likes instead of a paycheck as our salary, would we? So how do we relate Facebook likes and clicks to a financial result that will have an impact on business? Let's give it a try.

SEM Campaign: in this example, the campaign paid for 50,000 clicks at €0.05/click (CPM = €50). In the ad that we designed, since we want to see the impact on business, we run a promotion promising a discount coupon for answering one question about our product. This coupon was unique and could not be obtained in any other way. Three months later, the campaign reached the 50,000 clicks quota. Of those 50,000, 27,000 answered the question correctly and downloaded the discount coupon. At the point of sale, only 5,000 coupons were redeemed. The product sold for €2.00 with a 35 percent gross margin for the manufacturer. With all this information in our hands, we should be able to establish conversion ratios and the actual business result obtained from the SEM campaign. Let's see how it would look on a calculation sheet:

Table 3.3. - Transforming Communications Effects into Business Results

|  | Quantity or amount | Conversion ratios | Notes |
|---|---|---|---|
| SEM | 50.000 | | |
| Correct responses | 27.000 | 54% | |
| Redemption | 5.000 | 10% | |
| Retail price | 2,00 € | | |
| Product **gross margin** | 0,70 € | 35% | Retail price minus COGS and indirect costs |
| **Revenue** from paid clicks | 10.000 € | | Retail price per acts of purchase |
| Actual **gross margin** generated | 3.500 € | | Product gross margin per acts of purchase |

This table shows how to generate simple conversion ratios that will help you to manage and invest in future campaigns.

It is important not to confuse (which is very common to see, especially given the lack of a common ground in its definition) the use of the word *revenue*. For the purpose of our analysis and for the ROI Marketing Matrix, "revenue" is the inflow of money coming as a result of our marketing activities (also called gross revenues). It refers to the income generated mainly through sales (but it could be any of the revenue data mentioned earlier). For the money generated once the cash outflows (either cost of goods sold and indirect costs or marketing expenditures) are discounted from the revenues (gross), we will use the term *margin*—either "gross margin" in the case of revenues minus COGS and indirect costs or "net margin" (or return) in the case of deducting marketing expenditures. This last result will be the ROI of our marketing projects or campaigns.

Figure 3.7. - Revenues Versus Return

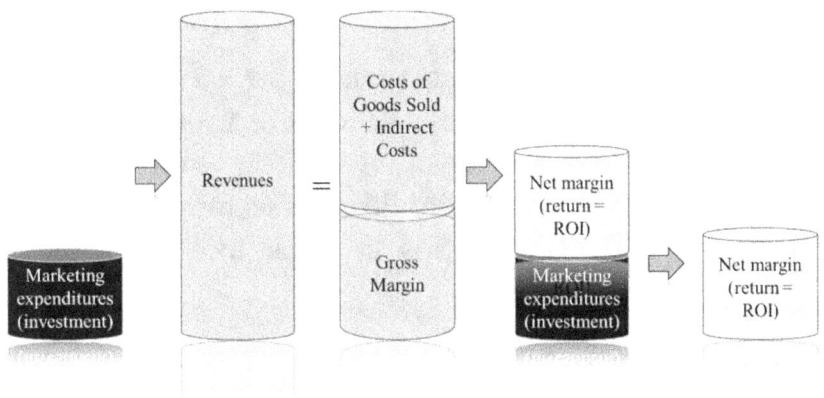

We previously said that our criteria should meet certain standards (simple, robust, reliable, and accepted). We need to prove that this sample of fifty thousand clicks and the conversion ratios derived from them would be valid for any sample in the future. For this, we need to prove that they are statistically relevant. Meaning, is the margin of error and level of confidence of this sample acceptable? In this example, the target segment size is 750,000 consumers. If this is the population and our sample is 50,000, what is its margin of error and level of confidence? Upon typing "sample size calculator" into a search engine, I found plenty of options to work with. One of them shows me that for this population and sample, the margin of error is 0.82 percent (steep distribution) and the confidence level is beyond 99 percent (high probability of repeating the same distribution if data collection is repeated on a duplicate sample). We could therefore comfortably say that this is a representative sample of our population from which we can extrapolate valid conclusions after compensating for the margin of error.

If these figures are accepted, then we have a solid starting point from which to calculate the ROI of this campaign and plan our future ones. Of course, with our next campaign evaluation, we should contrast these results and adjust our conversion ratios in order to minimize our margin of error.

*Social Media Group:* with social media, the quest for setting conversion ratios is a bit more complicated. For the purpose of illustrating this example, in this case, we will assume that we are not able to include a coupon or any other way of certainly demonstrate a conversion through redemption. How do we establish a cause-effect relationship between the traffic and interactions on our social media and its impact on business variables, such as sales? If we think of the chain of effects (expected or real) that comes after somebody enters our social media group, we could picture it as follows:

Learn about the group => consider it interesting to find out more => get into it => interact (subscribe, comment, "like," tag, talk about it, et cetera) => influenced by it, reconsider the relationship with the brand and/or product. Be more inclined to choose or prescribe it as an option => reach a sales channel => buy it

*What* part of any act of purchase can we attribute to the social media? If we do not have any historical cases or statistical info, we will have to set that criterion we spoke about earlier. How can we do it? We can ask. It is important that we set a scale of possible answers that will allow us to comprehend a full range of options for the consumers while also giving the project evaluation the chance to gather the full range of possible influences (usually 1 to 10 works out fine). What should we ask? There could be several ways to ask. Here are some examples:

- What part of your purchase was due to your interaction in our Facebook group?
- How do social media influence your purchasing decisions?
- What was the main driver of your purchase of today? (In this case, the evaluator should set a menu of options in addition to a scale of influence.)
- How did you find out about us?
- Et cetera

*When* should we ask? During the time frame of our evaluation:

- at the cashier in exchange for a free sample
- in the loyalty program's usual channels of communication
- on the very same Facebook group
- from previous market research or surveys
- Et cetera

*Whom* should we ask? It is clear that in this case, we have a self-segmented target. The fact that they reach the social media means they are interested and are therefore our core group. If we want to prove the influence on the act of purchase, we can only ask buyers and/or potential buyers that interacted with our social media.

*How* are we going to collect the data, and *how* many times do we have to ask? The digital era has brought many easy ways to collect data, even within massive segments. In this example, the screen interaction brings the opportunity to collect the information by way of a questionnaire or survey. Regarding how many times we are going to ask, it depends on the size of our population (target group, segment, et cetera). But we should ask as many times as necessary to reach an accepted margin of error and level of confidence. As a standard, we could say that a 5 percent margin of error and 95 percent level of confidence is enough and generally accepted (but remember, you'd better ask previously what would be acceptable for your direct reporting, as this will save you time and will put you in a good position to discuss the results rather than the methodology while reporting).

Notice the use of the 3WH checklist on the above data-collection plan.

There is a general misconception about what margins of error and confidence levels are. It is clear that the larger the margin of error and the smaller the level of confidence, the less acceptable or valid our conclusions would be. The smaller the margin of error desired, the larger the sample that needs to be taken to achieve it. For error, we understand it to be any deviation from the true answer. But what is the true answer? In the case of marketing, the "true" answer may be impossible to find; after all, if marketers knew it, whatever they did would be successful. Even if they asked 100 percent of the population, marketers still wouldn't be able to have the certainty of the answer because of the unpredictability of consumers' behavior. But the fact that it would be almost impossible to find the "true answer" doesn't mean that we cannot carry out an adequate analysis serving the purpose of measuring the impact of marketing. In fact, by finding a significant statistic, we are securing the use of a method that will provide information with controlled deviations in a relevant and rigorous manner. This way, we build the credibility and robustness of the conclusions extracted from the data.

On the other side, we have the confidence level (or interval), which sometimes is a bit more complicated to understand; it's also the one more often misused (especially in the media). Let's assume that we see the results of a conference poll stating that we have a 5 percent margin of error and a 95 percent confidence level. One common basic mistake is to think that the confidence level is the "negative" of the margin of error, and therefore, the addition of the two should always give 100 percent: margin of error (5%) + confidence level (95%)= 100%. This is very wrong. For the purpose of marketing analytics, an error consists on random and unpredictable deviations of answers between replicated questions. It is about how far apart the different answers are from the mean answer. It talks about how "high" or "low" our

Gauss bell would be. It refers to the density of answers within a range of values (normal distribution).

The confidence level refers to the probability of that normal distribution (proportion of answers) being repeated if the questions were asked to more replicable samples of the population. Therefore, it could be perfectly feasible that we would have an 11 percent margin of error and a 99 percent confidence level in our set of data.

Once we have these two figures (margin of error and level of confidence), we want to correct/compensate our conclusion with them (subtracting the margin of error and multiplying by the confidence level). Although this correction may not be completely accurate, we are "punishing" the data and obtaining a more conservative, rigorous, and acceptable figure. This is certainly much better than not having done anything at all. If this process is repeated through time, it will become much more assertive and acceptable.

With the final result, we will be able to infer a direct number (or a portion) of the acts of purchase that can be attributed to our social media group. Is this 100 percent certain? Certainly not, but we have asked the right people the right question from a statistically relevant sample of the population, treating the numbers in a very conservative way, knowing our margin of error and discounting for it.

Continuing with our social media example, it would work like this:

Target group (population): 750,000 people

Sample (responses) needed to have at least a consented 5% margin of error and 95% confidence level: 384 answers

Responses obtained: 450 answers (better than what was previously defined as an acceptable margin of error)

Significant estimation of impact: 5% (measured from actual responses. Meaning that after correcting by the margin of error, the mean value of weighted responses is 5 percent. It represents the part of the act of purchase that could be attributed to this social media event in particular)

The estimation of impact was done across a scale, as previously suggested, of 1 to 10. The survey covered a full set of possible influences from zero influence to an "I wouldn't have bought it if it wasn't for the social media" (act of purchase determinant). This means that the degree of influence of 5 percent could be applied to the full sales volume, in this case to estimate the impact of social media on sales.

If we build a case using the ROI Marketing Matrix and continue evaluating marketing projects throughout time, we will be able to correct our ratios, adjusting them and making them more accurate along the way.

## Closing Points

- Set up your objectives thoroughly in all four dimensions of measurement (messages, interactions, costs, and revenues).
- Focus on delivery rather than on execution.
- Establish a cause-effect relation between marketing and its financial impact on the business.
- Plan your data collection. Use the "3WH" checklist.
- Assign a monetary value to marketing performance indicators.
- Validate all your criteria prior to using them in the ROI Marketing Matrix.
- Plan your ROI Marketing Ladder.
- Keep track of all your investments (marketing expenditures until you prove a net return) and affected costs (those impacted by the project)
- Don't forget to work your ROI Marketing Ladder all the way.

# Part 2
# ROI Marketing Matrix: How to Use It

# Chapter IV
# ROI Marketing from Theory to Practice

## Overview

Part 1 of this book made reference to the theory behind the ROI Marketing analysis and the methodology of the ROI Marketing Matrix. Measuring the financial return of marketing investments is then quite simple:

**Align and Set Objectives** — 1
- ✓ Positioning
- ✓ Education
- ✓ Interactions (on & off trade performance)
- ✓ Business (cost savings, cost avoidance, sales, and other revenues)

**Plan to Measure** — 2
- ✓ Define performance indicators and period of impact
- ✓ Plan data gathering
- ✓ Relate project inputs to business outputs
- ✓ Convert business impact to money generated by marketing

**Measure, Analyze, and Plan Again** — 3
- ✓ Calculate ROI
- ✓ Establish benchmarks
- ✓ Use key learnings
- ✓ Correct inefficiencies
- ✓ Use marketing as an investment portfolio for future planning

The best way to portray the relationship between these three steps is as a cycle. There is always a first cycle that needs to be completed. This one may seem the most complex and raise most of the initial questions as to whether calculating ROI is or is not possible in marketing. Defining accepted standards is the main challenge at the beginning. Once the first cycle is completed, companies will have an initial set of data and a practice that will make it much easier to complete the second cycle and the following ones. The first cycle defines indicators, data collection methods, relations and correlations, and conversion criteria and ratios. The second and following cycles can then use and perfect all these parameters. The initial effort to find consensus and proper measures will not have to be made repeatedly. Once the methodology is accepted and if all ROI Marketing guidelines are followed, robustness and credibility will grow with each evaluation.

The following diagram shows this relation in a clearer way:

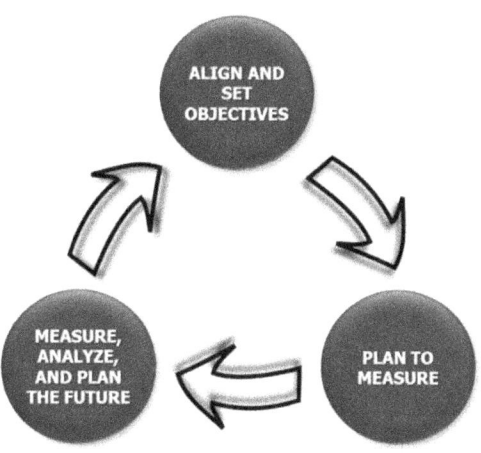

However, when it comes to implementation, especially the first time, the process of carrying on these activities may become intricate and, in some cases, seem impossible to achieve. In this part of the book, the reader finds a systematic elucidation as to how to put into practice the theory previously explained. During their many years of experience, the author and ROI Marketing Institute have gone through several different cases, in a variety of industries, under different scenarios, starting from completely diverse situations in the quest to figure out the ROI of marketing. Companies from all sectors, including but not limited to pharmaceuticals, insurance, fast-moving consumer goods, home appliances, and construction supplies, gave the ROI Marketing Institute the possibility to experience ROI marketing firsthand, while helping companies to set objectives, plan to measure and calculate the ROI of Marketing, setting the milestones for further analysis, and aiming to plan marketing more efficiently and with more accountability for the future.

## Table 4.1. – ROI Marketing Matrix Framework

| | | Stage | Action | Tools to use |
|---|---|---|---|---|
| **ROI MARKETING MATRIX** | **ROI Marketing Cascade** | Business Alignment | Establish congruence between marketing and business goals facing sustainability at three levels: economic/financial, social and ecologic | Joint analysis and validation with higher instances |
| | | Setting objectives | Define performance indicators, period of impact and measurement, sources of data, method of data collection, etc. | 3WH Check list |
| | | Marketing Strategy | Establish the marketing strategy for the year including global objectives | Marketing Plan |
| | | Marketing Tactics | Establish the different projects that will aim to achive the marketing plan goals | Marketing Plan |
| | | ROI Validation | Verify financial return feasibility | ROI Sensitivity Analysis. Historical data |
| | **ROI Marketing Ladder** | Data gathering | Collect all necessary information to verify marketing plan impact on communications and on business | Define during the objective set up (Questionnaires, surveys, etc.) |
| | | Relating | Establish a cause-effect relationship between communications performance (project inputs) and business impact (project ouputs) | Correlation methods (control groups, redemption, trend line analysis, etc.). Own data |
| | | Converting to money | Establish the monetary value of communication impacts | Conversion ratios. |
| | | ROI calculation | Define the financial return of marketing investments | ROI Formula (net margin/investments) |
| | | Conclusions | Set criteria for future planning | Benchmarks, marketing investment porftfolio |

Part 2 walks the reader, by using real-life examples and plausible scenarios, through possible ways of implementing ROI Marketing in any organization, showing barriers and enablers, how problems were solved, and the outcome (sometimes unexpected) of using ROI Marketing.

## How Close Is My Company to Implementing ROI Marketing?

This question may be expected to arise since the reader got his or her hands on this book. After reading part 1, it should be a bit clearer whether any organization is close to or far away from implementing ROI Marketing. Some indicators can pinpoint how far an organization is from determining the ROI of its marketing efforts. The following chart shows the degree of alignment, for any given organization, to an ROI Marketing organization (one being the furthest away and eight the closest):

Figure 4.1. – Organization ROI Marketing Alignment

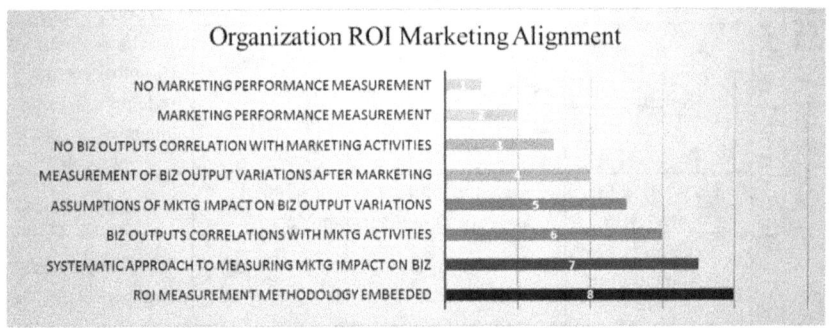

For all degrees of alignment, there is a clear position taken from the executive level regarding the role that marketing plays within any organization. If no marketing performance measurement is in place, it is clear that marketing is considered a marginal activity that will be undertaken only if disposable cash flow is available. In this case, marketing will most likely not be planned on a yearly basis but used as a reactive tool (for instance, if a competitor does something, the business will react, communicating in a counteracting manner) and surely with an unstable budget, which changes constantly as business evolves. On the other end of the scale, an organization that has an ROI measurement system in place is the closest to practicing ROI Marketing. As the ROI of marketing projects and/or campaigns is known, marketers will be able to analyze past results (ROIs) and compare them in order to plan future marketing expenditures as investments. Since there is an expected financial return from marketing (as much as there is for an investment in a new production line, a new product, a new ERP, and so on), the marketing budget should be allocated following the overall business goals (Is there a minimum expected return (ROI threshold) for any given investment at the corporate level, for instance?) and then treated as an investment portfolio.

While working on building the ROI Marketing Matrix around marketing plans, many issues and discussions will arise as performance indicators, relating criteria, and money conversion ratios are determined. Debates around these issues are normal, especially if an organization is trying to define them for the first time. Frequently, during the first year of ROI Marketing implementation, marketers could be working with ratios, criteria, and indicators with which they do not feel completely comfortable. However, marketing professionals will soon realize that it is better to have these ratios, criteria, and indicators in place than not to. After the first ROI cycle is completed, it will be obvious that this is an ever-evolving methodology and it improves with cases, inputs, and run-throughs. The more ROI Marketing is practiced, the more accurate and useful the methodology and philosophy will prove to be.

Of course, it will be much more difficult to prove the financial value of advertising than the financial value of a direct marketing campaign, but this does not mean that marketers should forego the effort to calculate both. The calculations may be done with different degrees of certainty and acceptance, but it is still much better to have them both than to have just one or none at all.

**Business Alignment**

Nowadays, it is difficult to conceive of a business that cares only about making money. As has been stated by many authors, the objective of a business is not to make money. Making money to a business is like breathing is to the human body. People do not wake up in the morning thinking: *My objective for today is to breathe continuously throughout the whole day*; yet, if people do not breathe, they die. A business that does not make money, if it is not an NPO (nonprofit organization), will sooner or later (it is just a matter of time) go bankrupt and die. So the objective of a business is not to make money; making money is part of its nature, its DNA. The goals of any modern business are of a three-part nature: economic, social, and environmental. The economic goals relate to *how much* money to make (rather than making money or not), and they depend on the expectations of the main stakeholders (shareholders most of the time). This *how much* could have a relation to the investment or to the time or simply be discretionary. The social goals aim to an aspect that can no longer be neglected. Whatever a business does, it will surely have an impact on society as a whole or on part of it. Business management does not have the opportunity to, and cannot afford the luxury of, making decisions that could or will have a negative impact on whatever part of society anymore. This social aspect of business refers to the direct impact on people and includes issues like child labor, social safety, safety at work, et cetera. The environmental goals are those that will have a direct negative impact on society if they are not amended. Matters like contamination, care of natural resources, the green effect, animal conservation, and so on, are all part of this element in the life of businesses.

The marketing of any business must deal with these facets. Consumers demand it. Economic sustainability is at stake if social and environmental sustainability are not well taken care of. Examples of large companies impacted by social mishaps abound, and the negative impact on the business never takes long to be seen.

An alcoholic beverage manufacturer client has, as part of its marketing code, the following manifesto:

- o Every effort should be made not to target minors or underage drinkers.
- o Activities must never depict or suggest people drinking heavily or rapidly or imply that such behavior is attractive or appropriate.
- o Abstinence must never be depicted in a negative light.

- Advertising will not depict the consumption of alcohol in an unsafe environment or as leading to social or sexual success.
- Promotions must encourage responsible drinking and must not promote excessive consumption.

These marketing codes are passed on to this client's agencies and suppliers, and they all must sign an agreement that they will adhere to and comply with this code while doing their creative and implementation jobs.

The marketing of this business is grounded on solid positive social-impact bases. If marketers failed to see and use this code while creating and executing their marketing plans, they would fail, even if they achieved the highest possible ROI with their marketing projects in the short term.

Aligning the three dimensions of sustainability (economic, social, and environmental) strengthens the future of the business overall. If businesses don't make money, they die. If stakeholders don't make the money they expect, they change their business/investment policies. If a business has a negative social or environmental impact, in the long run, it will also die as profits start shrinking because of the social response (not buying anymore) and the always more restrictive (in a positive way) international legal framework. All marketing projects and campaigns must be congruent with these three dimensions in order to be relevant and impactful for the business and to be meaningful to society.

**Setting Objectives**

Sometimes counterexamples show the concept better than a thousand words. Here is a list of real objectives set by real clients in real briefings received over many years of practice. Brands, specific names, and acronyms were removed to maintain confidentiality. We analyze them thoroughly and establish what each one of them is missing and how it could have been done properly.

What is wrong with these objectives?

1. To grow both "x" category and "brand" sales
2. To involve the target
3. To reach spontaneous awareness of 36 percent in target group
4. To launch the complete portfolio of products…
5. To make noise
6. To strengthen the relationship between "X" and its clients
7. To make the "brand" to be perceived as trendy
8. To incentive sales

Do they sound familiar? These objectives repeat the same concepts in different fashions but with the same type of enunciation. Although they may seem valid, they lack many important features necessary to be able to consider them as ROI Marketing objectives and are far from making it possible to measure the financial return of the marketing activities at stake. Again, we cannot blame science for asking the wrong questions.

What would they have to have in order to make it possible?

- *well-defined, measurable indicators*
- *a time frame*
- *achievable specific quantities*

In other words, the objective of "To grow both 'x' category and 'brand' sales" (the first one) should be enunciated the following way:

> To grow by at least 5 percent in value the overall category of "x" at the end of a six-month period. And to grow by at least 10 percent "brand" sales value in the same six-month period; in both cases compared to the same period of last year.

Do you see the difference? Now we know that we have to measure sales value during a six-month period for the overall market and for our product. We know that if we reach 4 percent growth of the category, we did not reach the objective and if we generate a 5.1 percent growth, we surpassed it.

These milestones of 5 and 10 percent respectively will come from a previously thought-out set of business objectives and/or sensitivity analyses. It is supposed that 5 percent is the necessary growth in value needed to support an overall business objective of, for instance, increased dividends by X percent. On another note, for example again, a 10 percent increase in sales value could be the necessary break-even point of the campaign.

The six-month period should also be the result of a previously contemplated (and validated) period of influence of the campaign or project at stake. This period will come from statistically relevant sources. Determining the period of influence of any marketing project is key to evaluating its ROI in a credible way. In order to define such a time frame, marketers have several tools at hand. Some ways to do so include the following:

1. *Internal consensus*—a relevant way and most likely the one with more chance of being accepted is internal questioning. Experienced people within the company can provide an educated guess about the potential impact of any given marketing project in business. Sales forces tend to be the ones more in contact with the market and generally the group of people that can come closer to the true impact of marketing on sales.

2. *Previous experiences*—events, direct marketing, advertising, point-of-sale activations, promotions, and a long list of other tools are used by marketers to perform their tasks. In some cases, questionnaires, surveys, and research are carried out, and the results can bring light to the period of influence of a given project.

3. *Industry standards*—category associations, think-tank groups, business school reports, and market

research are only some of the potential sources of information about the period of influence of marketing activities.

Keeping all these factors in mind, how should those objectives have been listed in order to be ROI Marketing driven?

Instead of
1. To grow both X category and "brand" sales  =>
   *To grow by at least 5 percent in value the overall category of X at the end of a six-month period. And to grow by 10 percent "brand" sales value in the same six-month period, in both cases compared to the same period of last year*
2. To involve the target      =>
   *To reach at least fifty thousand interactions across any of the brand's digital media by the end of the second quarter*
3. To reach spontaneous awareness of 36 percent in target group =>
   *To reach spontaneous awareness of 36 percent in target group at the end of the year*
4. To launch the complete portfolio of products… =>
   Launching a product portfolio is a strategic move; it is not an objective in itself. Innovation is most likely a tool to reach a business and/or marketing objective. If the company has developed a new product portfolio, it is clear that launching it is not an objective. The company already *has* a new portfolio; it has no option but to launch it.

5. To make noise =>
   *To generate at least one million impressions in gained media during the thirty days following the event*
6. To strengthen the relationship between X and its clients =>
   *To have at least 50 percent of our clients rating the relationship with our company as a partnership (instead of the other levels of: good supplier, a regular supplier, and just another supplier) on the questionnaires given after the event*
7. To make the "brand" to be perceived as trendy =>
   *To have at least 75 percent of questionnaire answers rating 4 or higher (on a scale of 1 to 5) the "brand" as trendy during the month following the campaign*
8. To incentive sales =>
   *To increase sales volume by at least 5 percent by the end of the third quarter*

Why are these objectives better enunciated? They have all the elements needed to be able to know for certain whether they have been achieved or not. They have measurable indicators with achievable specific quantities and are time framed. Let's take a closer look:

| Obj. | Measurable indicator | Achievable quantity | Time frame |
| --- | --- | --- | --- |
| 1 | Sales value | 5% and 10% | 6 months |
| 2 | Digital interactions | 50,000 | End of $2^{nd}$ quarter |
| 3 | Spontaneous awareness | 36% | End of the year |

| | | | |
|---|---|---|---|
| 4 | Not an objective | Not an objective | Not an objective |
| 5 | Impressions on gained media | 1,000,000 | 30 days after the event |
| 6 | Relationship rating | 50% as partner | After the event |
| 7 | Positioning rating | 75% rating 4 or higher | The month after the campaign |
| 8 | Sales volume | 5% | End of third quarter |

As many readers may have already noticed, not all of these objectives are business objectives. Neither do all of them have, by themselves, a clear connection to business variables, such as costs and/or revenues, but this does not mean that they are not complete. As we said at the beginning of the book, marketing has two dimensions: communications (messages and interactions) and business (costs and revenues).

It is clear that objectives 1 and 8 are business objectives while objectives 2 through 4 and 6 and 7 are communications objectives. While marketers are accountable for the communications results, they are seldom required, in the short term, to respond to business impact. That is why most of the time, especially in larger organizations; marketing divisions are far from sales divisions.

Fixing communications objectives is good and necessary. It is the first step to making it possible for the company to reach ROI measures. However, in order to do an ROI evaluation, it is always necessary to relate those communications inputs to business impacts. Once again, no money, no ROI.

Now it is time to think about specific objectives for each dimension of measurement: messages, interactions, costs, and revenues. As mentioned earlier, these are the four dimensions marketing can influence with a relevant effect at both levels (communications and business).

## *Message Objectives*

Messages can affect the way consumers and/or customers think about a brand or product and what they know about it particularly. What they think is technically known as "positioning" and what they learn refers to how consumers and/or customers can access the offer (where it is sold; what types of packaging is used; information about the variety of flavors, colors, or features; distribution; availability; new launches; et cetera). In this regard, during the planning phase, marketers should have defined the key performance indicators that can be related to business and converted to money. If key performance indicators are not related to business variables and monetized, at the end of the evaluation period, whatever result is achieved, it will be only related to the communications level, in other words, marketing as usual.

    Typical positioning message indicators include:
- brand awareness (spontaneous or induced)
- brand recall
- reputation

- marginal willingness to pay
- desired perception
- recognition
- soft segmentation (emotional attributes)
- etcetera

Typical education message indicators include:
- known product features
- known distribution points
- known points of sale
- competitive knowledge (difference with competitors, etcetera)
- hard segmentation (functional attributes)

A message objective should then be stated mentioning a given (expected) amount of any of the aforementioned indicators, that should be reached within a certain time frame. For instance:

*To have at least 90 percent of the target group knowing about the customer service call center number within a month after the point-of-sale campaign was launched.*

This is a clear objective with a measurable indicator and set time frame that can be related to a business variable (if knowing the phone number increases the number of calls and the number of calls reduces warranty claims, there is a cause-effect relation that has a direct impact on costs, a business variable).

There is a third type of message: messages that expect the target group to do something after the message has been received. Technically known as a "call to action" these messages work under the assumption that they will determine a certain behavior. These are the most commonly used and are shown as "results" of marketing projects and campaigns, but in reality, they are not a result of marketing but the input marketing generates. If the project is an event, for instance, the expected result should not be to receive a certain attendance but to achieve a given business impact as a consequence of such attendance.

Call-to-action messages drive behaviors and as such are the kickoff of interactions; therefore, their objectives blend with those related to these interactions. Interactions objectives are probably the most relevant, as their indicators are the ones marketers are most used to controlling and are those that could be more easily related to business variables.

Typical interaction indicators include:
- visits to a web page
- registration and affiliation
- attendance
- downloads
- samplings
- product tests
- quote requests
- likes
- tweets
- et cetera

An example of an interaction objective could be:

> *To have at least 10,000 respondents to the direct marketing campaign within the two-month period starting the day the campaign is mailed.*

Again, responses can be directly linked to a business impact if they are followed up and eventually turned into quote requests and ultimately into sales (revenues).

Finally, business objectives derive from business needs (generally and basically, reduced costs and increased profits). They are dictated by circumstances most of the time outside the marketing department (procurement, general management, boards, stakeholders, regulatory bodies, et cetera). The most common way to impact business variables from the marketing department is in a relative way: reducing existing costs, avoiding possible ones, and increasing current revenues that generate a profit.

Typical costs indicators are:
- churn
- warranty claims
- current marketing expenditures
- fines
- tax cuts
- etcetera

Notice that these indicators do not differentiate between the costs of doing marketing and the costs impacted by marketing, as they are both equally relevant to the business. One possible cost objective could be:

> *To reduce the overall marketing budget at year-end by 10 percent, keeping the same amount and type of executed projects.*

When it comes to revenue objectives, it works more or less the same but in the opposite way.

Typical revenue indicators are:
- sales value
- sales volume
- customer lifetime value
- act-of-purchase value
- donations
- etcetera

In the same way, a revenue objective could be:

> *To increase the value of each act of purchase by 15 percent during the three months following the campaign.*

Revenues contain profits (if they are higher than the costs held to generate them), and there is no further need to relate to business.

## Marketing Strategy

The issue of a marketing strategy in itself goes beyond the scope of this book. The marketing strategy represents the definition of the means that will allow a business to achieve its goals (business, social, and environmental ones). In most cases, at any given point in time, the marketing strategy is defined as part of the planning of the following year at least, and therefore, it will already be defined, in most cases, by the time marketers start thinking and working as ROI Marketing practitioners. It includes long-term, broad activities that need to be carried out to achieve those goals by defining the way products, prices, distribution, promotions, and communications will take place. Strategies affecting these areas can take different paths from defensive to developmental to aggressive, et cetera. Tactical marketing projects are born within these lines of action or policies. Each project shall have its own objectives that should be aligned with the overall broader goals and strategy. Marketing strategy comprises but is not limited to market research and SWOT analysis; a fundamental part of marketing planning shall also be a plan to monitor progress along the time line. This plan to monitor should include all ROI-related variables, including the plan to gather data and to relate communication inputs to business outputs and a credible, rigorous accepted way to convert those outputs to business variables (costs and revenues).

## Marketing Tactics

Efficient tactics rely on careful planning and excellent execution. Careful planning starts with a good briefing (the document that marketers use internally or with suppliers to express their objectives, needs, indicators, requirements, mandatories, et cetera, for any given project). A good briefing should include the right objectives (as stated above, at all levels: communications and business objectives); the intended investment (budget); and all relevant information needed for the party (internal or supplier) to perform the tasks necessary to achieve the goals.

An example will help us capture the point. The following briefing was given by a perfume manufacturer to its agency. All brand and company references have been removed for confidentiality purposes. It is a real brief as it was received:

*LAUNCHING OF FEMALE FRAGRANCE[1]*

*Antecedents:*
- *The company is one of the largest perfume manufacturers in the world but is lagging behind the leader at the local market.*
- *Fragrances launches are important and strategic to the brands.*
- *One year ago, the company launched its male fragrance that it is selling very well. It occupies the 7th place in the local male and female market (even though it is a male fragrance). Additionally it is one of the fragrances with higher accumulated growth.*

---

[1] Note from the author: all references to product variations have been removed for confidentiality purposes. They were included, along with a short description of their positioning, in the original.

*Current situation:*
*We will launch the new female fragrance in two phases:*
- *First phase: standard launching in July to the point of sale.*
- *Second phase: Christmas season launch*

*On the First phase, there will not be much but on the second, there will. For the Company, the Christmas launch is very important as it represents 35–40% of annual sales. In addition, for this campaign, the Company will do a launch pack that includes a giveaway (product or gift) with the fragrance. Christmas campaign is the push to keep high sales for the rest of the year.*

*Product:*
*The female fragrance will have three variations.*
- *Variation one*
- *Variation two*
- *Variation three*

*Company has colors and packing at the office for reviewing and checking how each variety is presented.*

*Consumer Profile:*
- *Young.*
- *Girls 18–25.*
- *Compulsive purchase carried out by trends, friends advises and youngsters' magazines.*

*Brand Value:*
(Note from the author: this space was left blank. They did not mention anything about it.)

*Positioning:*
(Note from the author: this space was left blank. They did not mention anything about it.)

*Communication Tone:*
*We have to be very careful with the communications tone. Especially regarding the bad interpretation that is sometime associated with the Brand. We have to talk always about seduction that it is the leitmotiv of the TV campaign.*

*Launching Date:*
*First phase: July.*
*Second phase: Christmas Campaign; October 1$^{st}$ thru January 6$^{th}$*

*Job to Do:*
*For the second phase, we want to do two promotions, one for the point of sales employees of one type of clients (106 points of sale), and one for the consumers of another type of clients. They will both coincide in time but not in target.*

*Delivery Timing:*
(Note from the author: a delivery time table was given by the client.)

There was no mention of the objectives or the intended budget to execute the project. Even the best project description would fail to start if it was not related to specific goals and to the available budget to execute the tasks at stake. Furthermore, even a successful project from the execution point of view, could be harmful to the company if its impact is not aligned with the overall business and marketing objectives. Without clear goals, it will be very difficult to know objectively whether the project was successful or not, in addition to the fact that meaningful planning will become almost an impossible task.

There are several types of available marketing tools that can reach a very broad range of possible communication and business objectives. Marketing is a rich discipline, and as such, it has a vast variety of resources marketers can use. However, marketing tactics should not only plan for execution of marketing tools and techniques but also for measuring the impact of those tools and techniques on the business. To do this, marketers will need to evaluate the project at the business level. Project ROI evaluation should never be considered a postactivity analysis but a planned set of processes that will make it possible to collect data during and after the project that can be related to business (costs and revenues) and to convert the information into monetary impacts.

From the ROI Marketing point of view, marketing tactics should always include a careful plan to:

1. Create a detailed *plan to collect the relevant information* (communication and business data, including but not limited to: impressions, GRPs, CTR, attendees, ratings, evaluations, affiliations, company records, industry information, et cetera).
2. Find detailed, conservative, robust, and accepted *criteria to relate communications inputs* (messages and interactions) *to business variables* (costs and revenues).
3. Define the *financial value of communication inputs* generated through the aforementioned relating criteria.
4. *Execute the activities* that will bring the expected results.

## ROI Sensitivity Analysis

The ROI Sensitivity Analysis is the tool that will help marketers to validate a project prior to the first money investment. It is the equivalent of determining the internal rate of return (IRR) of any business investment. The ROI Sensitivity Analysis serves the following purposes:

a) generates awareness about ROI in marketing as a way to transform it from an expense into an investment
b) builds internal credibility around marketing as a discipline
c) connects the notion of marketing influencing the business besides the communication

d) generates a necessary connection between marketing and sales division activities
e) validates a project from the financial perspective
f) minimizes the financial risks of marketing investments

In order to carry on the ROI Sensitivity Analysis, it is necessary to have a clear picture of communications and business objectives and the budget available for the project. Failing to do so means that a marketing project will be done without consideration of its influence and with a high uncertainty of its real impact on business.

The ROI Sensitivity Analysis is about finding the break-even point of a given project and figuring out whether this point is achievable with the available resources and project plan. It starts defining the impact needed on sales to pay back the investment and/or generate a profit. Given a sales margin, math will work out the quantity. The formula budget divided by net margin will tell the organization the minimum amount of sales needed to repay the marketing expenditure. If sales are higher, marketing will be generating profits. If sales are lower, marketing will be losing money for the business. Once this threshold amount is determined, marketers should question whether the project at stake is capable of generating the impact that will drive the marginal sales. The ROI Sensitivity Analysis should always have as a result 0 (zero), as the intention is to determine the break-even point (no losses, no profits).

Let's work it out with a real case from the insurance industry. (Numbers have been altered for confidentiality purposes)

|  | Average policy value | Value relative weight | Qty of insurance policies | Volume relative weight | Customer lifetime (in years) |
|---|---|---|---|---|---|
| Dental | 45,00 € | 3% | 60.000 | 18% | 3,33 |
| Health | 830,00 € | 48% | 200.000 | 59% | 6,18 |
| Accidents | 260,00 € | 15% | 20.000 | 6% | 8,41 |
| Liability | 580,00 € | 34% | 60.000 | 18% | 6,83 |

| Weighted average policy value | 444,25 € | | Campaign days | 360 |
|---|---|---|---|---|
| Weighted customer lifetime | 4,73 | | Gross margin per policy | 7,00% |

|  | Unique visits/day | Policies | Policy/visit conversion ratio |
|---|---|---|---|
| Own agencies | 4000 | 700 | 17,50% |
| Web page | 10000 | 200 | 2,00% |
| Loyalty program | 150 | 20 | 13,33% |

|  | Year 1 | Year 2 | Year 3 |
|---|---|---|---|
| Marketing campaign budget | 1.000.000 € | 1.200.000 € | 1.325.000 € |

| Expectantions: | Estimation from marketing | Expected visits during first year | New policies (expected based on current conversion ratios) |
|---|---|---|---|
| 1) increase in visits to agencies | 1% | 14.400 | 2.520 |
| 2) increase in web page visits | 5% | 180.000 | 3.600 |
| 3) increase in visits to loyalty program | 10% | 5.400 | 720 |

| Expectantions: | Year 1 | Year 2 | Year 3 |
|---|---|---|---|
| 1) number of marginal policy sales | 6.840 | 8.208 | 9.029 |
| 2) pondered gross sales | 14.372.002 € | 17.246.403 € | 18.971.043 € |
| 3) profit generated by marginal sales (1) | 1.006.040 € | 1.207.248 € | 1.327.973 € |

(1) profit = gross sales x % gross margin before taxes

|  | Year 1 | Year 2 | Year 3 |
|---|---|---|---|
| Profit/cost ratio | 1,006 | 1,006 | 1,002 |
| Break-even point (ROI close to zero) | 0,60% | 0,60% | 0,22% |

| Estimations | Company records |
|---|---|

Notes:
  a) Estimations of expected increase in visits is based on educated assumptions from past experiences.
  b) Estimations of the number of policies sold are of 20 percent growth of sales for year 2 and 10 percent growth on year 3.
  c) This ROI Sensitivity Analysis is based on the assumption that gross margin for each type of policy will remain the same during each year.

Having done the math and played with the assumptions, it is possible to reach an ROI that is close to zero. Then it is time to start posing the right questions. Those questions would be:

1. How can I determine if a 1, 5, and 10 percent increase in visits (to own agencies, web page, and loyalty program respectively) is possible with the planned project or campaign and/or available budget?
2. What happens if I raise or lower the sales increase in year two and three?

How can marketers obtain responses to these questions? There are several sources of data that can provide acceptable answers to them. They include but are not limited to:

- *Internal survey*—the company's own sales force is a good source of information. All surveys should be statistically relevant, meaning that it is not enough to ask one or two people in the sales force.

It should be posed to enough people to have a maximum of 5 percent margin of error with a 95 percent or higher level of confidence. Internal surveys are a good way to start building credibility around ROI Marketing. By asking, for instance, the sales force their opinion about a marketing project, marketers will be showing they are talking marketing beyond the communications boundary, preaching ROI Marketing, and supporting the concept that marketing is an investment that directly impacts the bottom line.

- *Company recor*ds—sometimes it is possible to ask the very same clients the project attempts to approach. During a series of training events that a client organized, one agency was able to ask what the influence of such training events on their purchase decision was. Here are the actual results:

| | |
|---|---|
| Population: | 40,000 (target size) |
| Responses to survey: | 725 |
| Margin of error: | 3.61% |
| Level of confidence: | higher than 99% |
| Weighted average response rate: | 7.05% |
| Corrected by margin of error & confidence: | 6.30% |

Customers gave this company the actual indication of influence of training events on their purchase decision. This information could be verified in future projects by repeating the same question and treatment of the data. Even the first measurement represents already valid data that an ROI Sensitivity Analysis could use in future projects.

- *Accepted standards*—industry associations, reputed market research, and benchmark cases are only few of the generally accepted sources of standards that are frequently available to corporations of all sorts.

With the ROI Sensitivity Analysis ends the Planning Cascade phase of the ROI Marketing Matrix. At this stage, marketers should already have a clear set of well-defined objectives and a plan (including data gathering, relating effect, and converting to money criteria) that leave them ready to work the plan in the field. This moment marks the beginning of the Execution Ladder phase, which starts with data gathering.

## Data Collection

If a marketing project passes the ROI Sensitivity Analysis test, it is time to start planning the execution with ROI in mind. In other words, to answer the question: what data and how am I going to collect the information needed to prove that objectives are met and to measure the ROI of the project?

As previously stated, there should be four sets of objectives: messages (positioning and education oriented), interactions (effectiveness of call to action), costs, and revenues. It is necessary to define the indicators that will show whether the objectives are met in each one of these measurement dimensions. It is also important to determine and collect whichever parameter will help marketers to figure out the monetary value of communications drivers. Finally, marketers must gather the information that will help to relate the effect of messages and interactions to costs and revenues. For all these needs, marketers should first work on identifying and validating key performance indicators, relating effects, and criteria to assign monetary value.

*Key Performance Indicators*
Having the right, measurable indicators is the only way to guarantee that a complete evaluation can be assessed. Marketers can have "to increase awareness" as an objective, but how can they measure awareness? Of course, there are accessible ways to do this in the current environment; therefore, the most important thing is to clearly define the indicators that will be used in the evaluation process. An example of this could be "to be rated above 7 on a scale of 0 to 10, by at least 50 percent of the target group, as the most comfortable brand of running shoes on the market." From this point on, marketers know that they will have to ask, in a statistically relevant sample, to rate the brand, one of these criteria being "comfort" through a scaled questionnaire.

*Relating Effect*
Following the above-mentioned positioning indicator as the most comfortable brand of running shoes would not have any value to the business when converted to money

if there is no definition of which acts of purchase were influenced by the marketing project. Most leading brands carry on several marketing activities at the same time, making it very difficult to determine which of all acts of purchase (or part of them) were due to the project being evaluated. It is imperative to establish criteria to isolate the influence of marketing on marginal sales. For this purpose, marketers have a full set of tools, especially after the digital eruption, potentiated by the fast evolution of mobile technologies. The question that marketing managers should pose is: which are the marginal sales, or part of them, that can be attributed to the marketing project being evaluated?

*Monetary Conversion*
It cannot get any simpler: no money, no ROI. Once the relation is established, it is necessary to mark the financial value of each variation of the pointed indicator. If comfort is the indicator at stake, marketers should determine what percentage of each running shoe purchase act is due to or determined by comfort and what is the monetary value of it.

The outcome of data gathering is the Data Gathering Plan, which is based on the 3WH (what, when, who, and how) checklist as part of the marketing tactics definition of the Planning Cascade phase. Here is a good example of a Data Gathering Plan for a project (see next page):

Table 4.2. – Data Gathering Plan

| Objective | What is the indicator that will show a change? | When can I collect the data that will indicate a variation on this indicator? | Who has the ownership of this data, and who can provide me the information I need? | How am I going to collect these data? |
|---|---|---|---|---|
| Positioning | Example: scale rating | Most likely during and after execution | Most of the time the target group | Example: questionnaires |
| Education | Example: test survey results | Most likely during and after execution | Most of the time the target group | Example: survey |
| Interaction | Example: visits | Most likely during and after execution | It usually comes from data collection methods | Example: CRM, stores' records, etc. |
| Costs | Example: warranty claims | After execution | Company records | Internally provided |
| Revenues | Example: sales | After execution | Company records | Internally provided |

**Relating Effects**

Some ROI methodologies preach the need for isolating the effects of the project in order to determine its impact. In reality, in marketing, it is very difficult to isolate the effects of a given project. The life of marketing starts with the product, its price, its distribution, and finally its communication and contact with the market. The touch points with the market are several, and marketing activities are usually executed or implemented at the same times, places, channels, et cetera. How can marketers know the actual impact of those activities on the business?

In ROI Marketing, the idea is to determine which part of any business impact (cost reduction, cost avoidance, or revenue generation, either long or short term) can be attributed to the marketing activity, project, or campaign. The way to attribute a given impact is by relating the marketing input (attendance, visits, registration, GRPs, CTRs, media exposure, et cetera) to the project first and then to a specific part of the business output. In ROI Marketing, marketing inputs must generate business outputs.

The relating process is probably the most relevant process in ROI Marketing. It is the one that will determine whether the results of the evaluation will be considered, used, and respected or not. It establishes a cause-effect relation between messages and interactions (communications level) first and costs and revenues (business level) later. Without relating, it is not possible to determine ROI.

As previously mentioned, communications inputs are the result, the consequences of project activities in the messages and interactions communications dimension. The fact that people come to an event should not be the intended result expected when the event is planned. An event should have certain objectives behind it:

a) *positioning objectives* (what the event organizer wants the attendees to think about the product or brand),

b) *education objectives* (what the event organizer wants attendees to learn about the product or brand),

c) *call-to-action objectives* (what the event organizer wants attendees to do in relation to the product or brand), and

d) *business objectives* (what the event organizer expects in terms of costs and revenues to happen after the attendees come to the event).

In many cases, marketers include objectives a) through c); this is marketing as usual. Very seldom do marketing tactics include business objectives in their plans. Rarely do marketers establish a relationship between communications input and business results. This connection, often desired but very infrequently delivered, is the key to the ROI Marketing philosophy. For this purpose, marketers need to go beyond marketing as usual when planning. It is not necessary to change the way marketing is being done; it is about adding the necessary steps to connect messages to interactions first and the two levels of marketing, communications, and business, later.

Connecting interactions to a given project depends greatly on the nature of the project. It is very easy to infer that a new purchase from a completely new customer through a direct marketing campaign is a direct result of the very same marketing campaign. It is much more difficult to directly relate a given behavior to a massive advertising campaign, for instance. However, the biggest challenge comes when marketing staff have to generate a relation between the communications world and the business world. For this purpose, marketers are forced to establish a cause-effect relationship between messages and interactions and the impact these inputs have on costs and revenues. Which methods could be used to do so? As previously mentioned, there are some standard and ad hoc ways that marketers can use to show such connections.

The most commonly used ways to relate communications to business include the following:

- *Trend line analysis*—One of the relevant concepts in technical analysis is that of the trend. A trend is nothing more than the general direction in which a variable is headed. A *trend line* is formed when a straight line can be drawn between two or more equivalent points on a two-axle graphic. It starts from when the actual move begins to be measured, and the more points it involves, the more reliable the trend. In marketing, the usual equivalent points are the average or media values of the variable at stake (usually sales or business variables that can be converted to money). The critical point from the

ROI Marketing point of view is the difference between the existing trend prior to the marketing project's execution projected in time and the way it evolves during and after the project has been executed. For this difference in trend line projection and actual measurement to be relevant, it is necessary that all variables remain the same before, during, and for as long as the measurement takes place. If there is any change (for instance, an overall market growth), the results should be compensated by the verified change. For instance, if the trend line shows that there is an increase in a sales trend of 10 percent and it is known that the overall market grew 3 percent, the actual growth that can be attributed to the project is 7 percent (10 percent growth minus 3 percent market growth = 7 percent growth attributable to the project if all other variables remained the same).

Notice that the following chart mentions "sales during the project impact time" and not "sales during the project execution." The reason for this is that ROI Marketing is about determining the impact of a marketing project on the business, regardless of whether the project is finished or not.

Figure 4.2. – Trend Lie Analysis

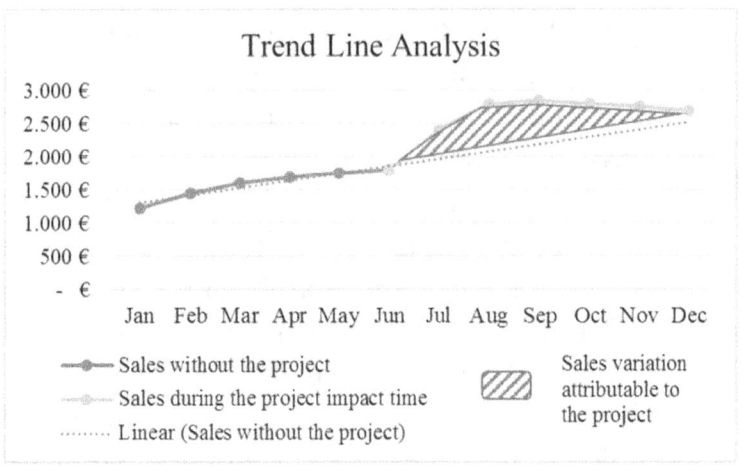

*Control groups*—A control group is a group separated from the rest of the target group so the marketing project being evaluated cannot influence the results. This isolates the project's effects on the business and can help to rule out alternative explanations to a given result. A control group evaluation is composed by two groups: the experimental group (the one that is exposed to the marketing project where changes are observed and recorded) and the control group (the one that is separated and not exposed to the project). If a change can be attributed directly and unequivocally to a project, there is no need to establish a control group. For the conclusions drawn from the results of controlled marketing projects to have validity, it is essential that the target groups assigned to the project be representative of the same population and be exposed to the same conditions. For instance, it would not be useful to implement a marketing project in the United States and compare its results to the German market, which was not exposed to the same marketing project. The reality, conditions, and even populations of these markets are completely different and whatever change is recorded could not be directly linked to the project with an acceptable degree of certainty.

*Company's own records*—In some cases, companies already have some relevant information that can be used as the basis to relate communication inputs to business. It is well known that the pharmaceutical industry has several tools to measure the impact of their marketing communication efforts. Insurance companies also have more sophisticated standards when it comes to seeing the input generated through marketing expenditures. Variables like customer lifetime value, conversion ratios, and attrition rates are only a few examples of these types of data. Furthermore, if a given company practices ROI Marketing, each measurement and evaluation serves as the basis for future measurement and evaluations.

- *Panel groups*—Panel groups (rather than focus groups, which are qualitative-results driven) are a great way to infer statistically relevant information needed to relate the two measurement levels. There are some great customer experience platforms (www.izo.es, for instance) that can nurture the data needed to establish a cause-effect relation. Panels are made of large samples of a population that respond to a set of questions. A large number of responses is collected in a statistically representative and relevant way.

- *Surveys and questionnaires*—Surveys and questionnaires are an easy and very competitive way to collect data in a statistical and indisputable way and can establish a cause-effect relation between what it is done on the communications level and what happens on the business level. But marketers have to be very careful and thoughtful when generating the questions. As previously mentioned, you cannot blame science if you are asking the wrong questions. The pharmaceutical industry is also very well known for doing questionnaires after conventions and congresses. Here are some real examples of questions asked after a pharmaceutical congress (respondents were asked to rate their experiences on a scale from 1 to 5):

    - "Please rate the reception process of the congress."
    - "Please rate the catering services during the congress."
    - "Was the content of this congress relevant to your profession?"
    - "Would you assist to more congresses of this type?"

- "Are you more or less likely inclined to prescribe solutions like the ones introduced in this congress?"

While these might be relevant questions to the marketing department in determining the overall satisfaction of attendees and the event's potential influence on future behaviors, there is very little connection between what is being revealed and its real impact on business. Is it really necessary to ask about the reception process? Could the organizer have noticed if the reception process was good or bad just by checking if there were lines, long waiting times, discourteous hosts, et cetera? What about the catering? What are the drivers of satisfaction in catering: quantity, quality, variety? How relevant is the answer to the business? Can it be connected to it? It is a common mistake to use the metrics of the last project in order to see evolution. This evolution might tell very little, if anything, about the evolution of the business and the impact the project represents for it. The last question is the one that gets closest to the possible influence of the congress on business, but due to legal limitations in many countries, the pharmaceutical industry is very restricted in getting to the point in their marketing efforts. Still, this does not mean that it cannot be done.

The last question tries to establish a connection between the communication effort and its impact on prescription sales. It cannot mention the specific drug because of legal limitations, but it is clear that all attendees to the event know which product is behind the content of the congress. "Inclination to prescribe" does not necessarily represent a conversion ratio. Of those "inclined" to prescribe, there might be some who will not actually do it. But there is a complementary way to determine the conversion between "inclination" and "actual prescription," and it is one already used heavily by the pharmaceutical industry: control groups. By leveraging questionnaires with further control groups, there is the possibility of establishing a cause-effect relation between a congress and prescription with a very low margin of error and a high confidence index. It all starts with the right questions and a bit of discipline and effort.

## Converting to Money

Once there is an accepted relating connection, it is time to give a monetary value to the communication indicators. If we consider a complex issue like "positioning," how can marketers establish a financial value for positioning their brand or product? As previously mentioned, it is not the same to have a goal of "to increase awareness" as "to be rated above 7 on a scale of 0 to 10, by at least 50 percent of the target group, as the most comfortable brand of running shoes in the market." So the question that marketers should ask is: how can I attribute, in an accepted and robust way, a financial value (in cash) to each positioning variation? Let's work through this example.

Runner market size
(yearly sales in volume): 100,000 pairs
Current volume market
share of the brand: 40%
Responses needed for a 99%
confidence level and a 3%
margin of error: 1812 responses

The question related to the comfort positioning effect on business, in this example, stated:

*"How much does comfort influence your decision to purchase your running shoes?"*

The answers were distributed as follows:

|  | 0% | 10% | 20% | 30% | 40% | 50% | 60% | 70% | 80% | 90% | 100% |
|---|---|---|---|---|---|---|---|---|---|---|---|
| # of responses | 0 | 112 | 90 | 120 | 115 | 213 | 454 | 285 | 233 | 190 | 0 |
| % of responses | 0% | 6,2% | 5,0% | 6,6% | 6,3% | 11,8% | 25,1% | 15,7% | 12,9% | 10,5% | 0% |
| Weighted % of influence (*) | 0% | 0,6% | 1,0% | 2,0% | 2,5% | 5,9% | 15,0% | 11,0% | 10,3% | 9,4% | 0% |

(*) Percentage of responses multiplied by percentage of influence

From these figures, marketers could calculate the average weighted percentage of influence without extreme values.

Average weighted % of influence: 6.82%
Margin of error: 3%
Weighted % of influence corrected

147

by margin of error: 6.62%[2]
Confidence level: 99%
Weighted % of influence corrected
by confidence level: 6.55%[3]

For each act of purchase variation during the time frame determined as the period of influence of the project, marketing managers of this company could confidently say that 6.55 percent of the revenues generated come from the positioning as a comfortable running shoe. Is this an exact figure? Certainly not. But it has been collected from a statistically relevant sample of the target group. It was weighted by relative responses. The margin of error was completely deducted for conservative reasons, and the overall result was compensated by the confidence level of the sample.

As previously stated, it is advisable to validate this criterion with the reporting level prior to starting to gather the data, as this will prevent later questioning of the methodology. If the criterion is not validated, marketers should keep working on an acceptable margin of error and level of confidence in order to determine a more reliable sample size.

It is important to remember that this 6.55 percent should be applied only to the variation previously identified as related (attributed) to the project. In addition, this percentage needs to be translated into money in order to

---

[2] 6.82 minus 3% margin of error.
[3] 6.62 multiplied by 99%.

allow marketers to calculate the ROI of the project at a later stage.

| | |
|---|---|
| Retail price (SRP) of running shoe: | €180 |
| Retail margin on SRP: | 50% |
| Distribution price of running shoe: | €90 |
| Manufacturer gross margin (without marketing expenditures): | 30% |
| Gross margin per running shoe: | €27 |
| Net contribution of the project to each marginal shoe sale: | €1.77 (6.55% of margin) |

Now marketing managers have converted positioning to money. Whatever money is invested in positioning could now be converted to money returned. In future projects influencing positioning as a comfortable shoe, marketers will already have a conversion ratio that could be used to make the evaluation a much easier task. Subsequent evaluation will fine-tune and improve this ratio, making it more credible and robust. As ROI Marketing becomes a standard practice within the organization, following evaluations of similar projects will start improving the efficiency of measurement processes and the accuracy of relating and converting criteria.

## ROI Calculation

One of the most commonly repeated mistakes is stopping the process at the revenues dimension. Revenues are not returns, the same way sales are not 100 percent profits.

One client from the insurance industry once told me that thanks to the loyalty program they had in place, they were able to generate an extra €130 million in policies, and because of this, they knew the loyalty program was very successful; this is a dangerous approach, however. What is this conclusion missing to be certain of the success of the program?

1. By this statement, it is assumed that 100 percent of extra sales come from the loyalty program. It would be necessary to find out in which way they knew that this was an exclusive result of the project, meaning, if the loyalty program were not in place, they would have done none of those €130 million.
2. Nothing was said about other business alignment factors (social and environmental impact, for instance).
3. The fact that it generated sales does not mean that it generated profits. Let's assume that insurance has a gross margin of 40 percent. If the investment on the loyalty program was higher than €52 million, then the project was making the business lose money in the short term.

The calculation of marketing ROI is straightforward. The return on any marketing investment is the net margin (gross margin minus marketing expenditures/investment) obtained. In order to express it as a percentage, it is necessary to divide the gross margin by the marketing investment and multiply it by 100.

$$\frac{\text{Gross margin} - \text{Marketing investment}}{\text{Marketing investment}} \times 100 = \text{ROI}$$

The complexity arises when it comes to determining which part of the gross margin is related to the marketing project, what the actual marketing investment (expenditure) is, and how the impact of marketing on business variables is determined. The way marketing impacts costs and revenues is calculated, its feasibility, and its robustness are fundamental to determining credibility and acceptability of the overall process. Congruence with business goals, consistency throughout the processes, completeness of data collection, and the accuracy and conservativeness of it should drive the ROI Marketing philosophy. Marketers (agencies and advertisers) are used to reporting marketing performance measures that in most cases reflect quantitative variables, but those variables are seldom meaningful for the financial business if left alone (as usually happens). What does one point of GRP (advertising gross rating point) mean for the bottom line of the business? Marketing reports also include soft variables, such as brand awareness for instance. Nobody doubts brand awareness is fundamental to the success of any product's bottom line; however, how this brand awareness impacts it and when is hardly, if ever, shown. Setting a unique measurement standard (ROI) across all marketing investments (advertising, grassroots, direct marketing, etc.) minimizes the fuzziness of marketing reports to business executives while building the credibility and relevance of marketing as a division.

On the running shoe example mentioned earlier, the calculation of ROI would work as follows:

| | |
|---|---|
| Net contribution (gross margin) per marginal sale of running shoe: | €1.77 |
| Brand market share in volume: | 40% (40K pairs) |
| Margin generated positioning the product as a comfortable shoe: | €70,800 |
| Investment on positioning (assumption for the example sake): | €90,000 |

$$\textbf{ROI} = \frac{\text{gross margin} - \text{investment}}{\text{Investment}} \times 100 =$$

$$\frac{€70{,}800 - €90{,}000}{€70{,}800} \times 100 = \textbf{-27.12\%}$$

This means that for every €100 investment, the advertising company loses €27.12. Assuming the advertising positioning campaign was massive enough to have impacted the majority of the target group.

However, marketing managers should not be deceived by this result. This calculation is based on forty thousand pairs of shoes, which represents the sales of one year. If sale volume is increased, negative ROI will be diminished. If marketing investment decreases, negative ROI will decrease. In addition, there are a whole set of intangibles that should be gauged. Intangibles are value that cannot be translated into money without considerable cost and most of the time, longer than acceptable time frames of influence, but they can determine whether a project should be maintained or not. Business alignment comes into place at this stage, and there are many other factors to consider prior to deciding if the project should be continued or not. A true ROI Marketing ambassador would also ask further questions like:

- How many pairs of shoes should the company sell in order to make this project feasible from the financial point of view?
  Answer: 50,848. By dividing the total investment (€90,000) by the gross margin per pair of shoe sold (€1.77), marketers can establish the break-even point (same way it is done through the ROI Sensitivity Analysis in the planning phase).
- Is this an obtainable amount for the given circumstances?
- Can this number of pairs be sold with the current level of investment?
- How much would marginal investments increase sales and reduce negative ROI?

In some cases, it is also necessary to use caution to avoid double counting the cost of marketing. Many companies include marketing investments as part of the cost of goods sold (COGS). Therefore, the gross margin already accounts for marketing investments. If this is the case, overall marketing investments should be deducted from the COGS, obtaining a new gross margin rate (higher). This new gross margin rate should then be used to determine the impact of any marketing project from which the investment at stake during the evaluation process (the project or campaign) should be deducted. In other words:

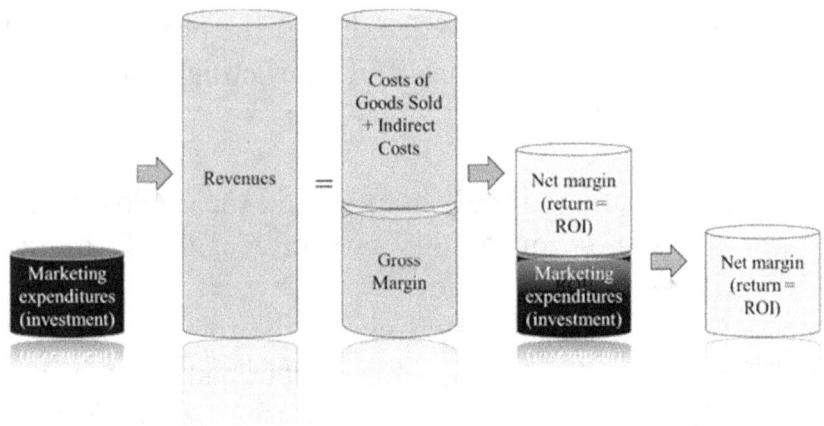

If COGS includes marketing investments, deducting marketing expenditures from the gross margin would deduct the same cost/investment twice.

In our example, if the 30 percent gross margin already included marketing investments as cost of goods sold in its calculation, then the investment was already accounted for. How then can marketers determine the ROI of positioning? By calculating which part of the overall marketing investment was dedicated to positioning, deducting it from the original gross margin, and applying the new margins.

In our example:

| Item | Figure | Calculation |
|---|---|---|
| Cost of goods sold (COGS): | €63/pair of shoe | €90 distributor price minus €27 gross margin |
| Positioning marketing investment: | €90,000 | Assumption in this case |
| Positioning marketing investment per pair of shoes: | €2.25 | €90,000 divided by 40,000 pairs sold |
| Overall marketing investments (all marketing plan activities): | €300,000 | Assumption in this case |
| Marketing investment per pair of shoe: | €7.50 | €300,000 divided by 40,000 pairs sold |
| New marketing investment discounted investments in positioning | €210,000 (€5.25 / pair of shoes) | €300,000 - €90,000 |
| New gross margin | 32.5% (€29.25 / pair of shoes) | €27 (original margin) + €2.25 (positioning marketing investment) |
| New gross margin generated by positioning | €1.92 (€76,800) | 6.55% of €29.25 (€1.92 multiplied by 40,000 pairs sold) |
| New corrected ROI | -14.67% | €90,000 minus €76,800 divided by €90,000 multiplied by 100 |

A deeper and more thorough analysis shows an ROI that is close to 50 percent better than the original one. ROI marketers should think this way and consolidate data robustness through a holistic view of marketing and its financial impact on the business.

**Conclusions**

Finally, the ROI Marketing Matrix is a methodology that will help marketers (and non-marketers) to determine the financial return on investments of marketing projects of different natures at any time. It is one simple way to embrace ROI Marketing as a standard to show the value of marketing for any company or organization. No money, no ROI does not mean that marketers cannot influence and generate more value out of their marketing activities. Alignment is not only about shareholders' expectations. It is about *all* stakeholders' expectations. This means that the expectation to be satisfied goes far beyond profits and is not limited to ownership and governance but extends to clients, employees, partners, and society as a whole as well. Marketing projects should not be an exception to this; therefore, it is advisable (for the sake of marketing sustainability within businesses) that marketers think of aligning marketing activities to a series of interests that should be contemplated when planning each project. Since the analysis goes beyond profits, marketing professionals should think in terms of value generation. Value can be defined by short-term and long-term impact. It should also be considered from the three scopes of sustainability mentioned earlier: economic (profits), social (impact on society), and ecological (impact on the environment). Once a project has been evaluated, as part of the final report, marketers should include not only financial measures but also nonfinancial, soft data influencing those other scopes. For marketing managers, at the beginning, this complex business alignment point of view may seem far from their responsibility or interests, but the higher in the hierarchy the person receiving the evaluation report is, the more relevant these aspects become. All marketing projects should be aligned with the business overall.

Reviewing business alignment will also give marketers the chance to improve future projects and use past key learnings to increase the impact of marketing on the life of the business and beyond. This review process will also help to establish benchmarks and good practices that could be transposed to other projects. Past evaluation reports should be the basis for planning and evaluation of future projects, especially if they are of the same nature.

The ROI Marketing Matrix provides the opportunity to think and plan marketing activities in a holistic way. It all starts with a good set of well-defined objectives and continues with a careful planning that not only includes the implementation of the activities that will deliver the messages and interactions but also the data gathering and its analysis to evaluate the project from the ROI perspective during and after execution. Finally, it delivers a common standard of measurement (ROI) to evaluate and gauge the contribution of each project to the business overall, short and long term. Once this ROI standard is delivered across different marketing projects, marketers will be able to compare apples with apples, while talking about different types of projects and channels. Marketing now has a full set of investment portfolios that make it possible to make much sounder business decisions when planning in the near future.

However, the process is not finished yet. There is one final step in ROI Marketing that could determine the future of ROI Marketing within an organization: reporting. All marketing evaluations should finish with a report. Reporting can occur at many different levels within the organization (and outside of it as well). Here are a couple of pieces of advice to take into consideration when reporting ROI:

- o If results are negative, make sure you also bring a way to overcome the bad news, including a way to change the project if done again or an alternative project that aims to reach the same goals the first one was designed for.

- o If results are positive, make sure you show the information sources, criteria chosen to relate communications to business, conversion to money, and all necessary means to make the conclusions indisputable, and focus on ways to benchmark and replicate the good results.

# Appendix A
# How to Get Started

## How to Get Started

There could be many roads leading to integrating ROI Marketing into any organization. ROI Marketing Institute (www.roimarketinginstitute.com) offers a variety of different approaches that can help professionals and corporations of any kind to become ROI Marketing practitioners through:

- *ROI Learning*: ROI learning is the training center where professionals and organizations can acquire the first contact and knowledge about measuring properly the return on investment of marketing projects and campaigns. It is a workshop that can be done at the premises of any company or organized externally. There are also regular open workshops where anybody can join throughout the year.

- *Professional and Corporate Certifications*: ROI certification is intended for those organizations and/or professionals interested in achieving the top standard for ROI Marketing measurement knowledge and practices. It proves that the certified bodies or professionals have acquired a set practices that, if applied properly, will lead to determine the ROI of Marketing projects and campaigns in a reliable and robust way.

- *Systems Integration and Implementation*: all good practices need systems that can guarantee implementation. Measuring the financial return of marketing is no exception. ROI Marketing Institute consultants can help companies to integrate or create systems that will ensure those practices are incorporated into the standard operating procedures.

- *Consulting:* it is a service intended for organizations that would like to have an external source of checking their marketing processes regularly or punctually, throughout a given period, aiming to determine the financial return of specific marketing projects or campaigns, or the level of adoption of return on investment measurement practices.

For more information, check www.roimarketinginstitute.com

www.ingramcontent.com/pod-product-compliance
Lightning Source LLC
Chambersburg PA
CBHW071800200526
45167CB00017B/525